ANGER CONTROL AND CONFLICT MANAGEMENT FOR KIDS

A Learning Guide for the Elementary Grades

Terri Akin

Susanna Palomares

Cover Design: Dave Cowan

Edited by: Dianne Schilling

Copyright © 2011, Innerchoice Publishing • All rights reserved

ISBN – 10: 1-56499-078-5

ISBN – 13: 978-1-56499-078-5

INNERCHOICE Publishing
15079 Oak Chase Court
Wellington, FL 33414

www.InnerchoicePublishing.com

Peace is not won by those who fiercely guard their differences, but by those who with open minds and hearts seek out connections.

—Katherine Paterson
The Spying Heart

Contents

Helping Children Deal Constructively with Anger and Conflict

Everyone gets angry, and everyone gets involved in conflict. Both are normal human experiences and often one leads to the other. Anger can lead to conflict, and conflict can lead to anger. They generally go together and it's hard to tell which came first anger or conflict. Indeed, it's often difficult to tell them apart. It's only natural then that the teaching of the skills and awarenesses that lead to the ability to effectively managing these powerful emotional events be taught together. Children need to learn effective ways to control, express, and release their anger and strategies for dealing with the conflicts that inevitably arise in life.

The activities in this curriculum guide are designed to demonstrate to students the power of approaching anger and conflict with a win-win attitude, and to teach them a number of basic pro-social strategies for managing anger and resolving conflict. The experiential group activities included in this guide examine the nature of anger and conflict as well as their causes, effects, and resolutions. A unique Sharing Circle and role-play process builds into the learning experience repeated opportunities for behavioral rehearsal.

In order to manage anger and resolve conflicts, students must remain open, flexible and creative. The long-range goal is to empower students to continue seeking creative, positive strategies for resolving conflict and managing their anger away from the classroom or group, in their everyday lives, and to carry those skills with them into adulthood.

Because so many influences in their lives teach otherwise, powerful approaches and consistent intervention are needed to teach children positive, social and emotional skills. Practice makes perfect. Repeated exposure to positive alternatives, consistent reinforcement, and practice. Lots of practice!

Implementation of the activities and numerous opportunities to participate in the Sharing Circle and role-play process will produce student gains in:
- self-awareness
- self-management
- communication skills
- problem-solving skills
- use of pro-social conflict and anger-management strategies

Learning together in a classroom or counseling session makes it easier to internalize the skills, strategies, and methods of anger control and conflict management. We all are social beings designed by our long evolutionary history to learn our interactive behaviors with others. The activities in this book are designed to actively engage the students with each other in applying knowledge, solving problems, communicating, cooperating, and relating experiences to their own lives. Armed with these skills children can become confident self-governing problem-solvers able to deal more effectively with anger and conflict and contribute to society with the goal of a better future for us all.

How the Guide Is Organized

The activities presented in the first section of the book engage students in defining anger and conflict, distinguishing between the languages of anger and conflict escalation and the vocabulary of peaceful resolution, and examining how certain verbal and nonverbal behaviors tend to escalate or de-escalate both anger and conflict. Key communication skills — active listening and I-statements — are introduced and practiced.

In this section nine distinct conflict-resolution strategies are presented. Each strategy is explained and illustrated on a set of reproducible student handouts. The activity "Learning Conflict Resolution Strategies," provides a step-by-step process for teaching these strategies.

Additional activities in this section scrutinize specific strategies, provide additional practice in using the strategies, and examine concepts such as cause and effect, perspective, and cooperation — all designed to increase student understanding of anger and conflict and foster insights into the complex nature of each.

The second activity section, "Sharing Circle and Role-Play Topics," begins on page 107, and is devoted exclusively to a unique process that enables students to rehearse the nine conflict-resolution strategies presented in the first section of the book and to develop and test strategies of their own. The Sharing Circle topics structure contexts within which behavioral rehearsal can occur. Each topic approaches the subject of conflict from a different perspective, and the incidents, which the students role-play, are developed from their own experiences.

How to Use the Activities

The activities, Sharing Circles, and role-plays in this book have been designed to 1) build a base of awareness, understanding, and skills required for anger management and conflict resolution, 2) give students practice using a variety of strategies for managing anger and resolving conflict, and 3) create opportunities for students to apply those strategies to real-life problems and conflicts.

The activities, including the Sharing Circle and role-play topics, may be implemented with considerable flexibility. However, before students begin participating in role plays, they should be familiar with some or all of the nine conflict resolution strategies presented in this curriculum. Lead the activity, "Learning Conflict-Resolution Strategies," on page 85, and distribute the strategy handouts. Ask the students to refer to the strategies when they brainstorm alternative resolutions to the conflicts they dramatize.

The activities in the book are divided into two sections. The first section, entitled Group Activities, is devoted to awareness, skill development and practice. The second section, Sharing Circle and Role-Play Topics, contains activities that are designed to supplement those in the first section. They also provide students with expanded opportunities to engage in discussion and presentation which allows them to better understand themselves and to share those understandings with others to promote higher levels of self awareness, social interaction, and mastery.

We encourage you to adjust and modify activities to suit the ages, ability levels, cultural/ethnic backgrounds, and interests of your students. You will know best how to maximize the appropriateness and impact of each activity, so please do so. The activities that are specifically designed for young children are indicated in the subheading on the activity page.

Theory and Background

Children and Resiliency

Children whose resiliency skills are strong can generally deal constructively with conflict. Children find conflict management difficult when they are not aware of how they feel, are unable to understand the needs and feelings of others, and doubt their own effectiveness.

Consider this example: Corey gets to sleep very late because an older brother is playing music loudly. The next morning, he gets up late and misses breakfast. He is tired, hungry and generally irritated. All of this could happen to anyone, but Corey is groping his way into a new day with little awareness of how he feels physically or that he is resentful of his brother for keeping him up late. With awareness of these feelings buried, Corey is practically guaranteed to get into a conflict sometime during the day, and is much more likely to handle the conflict aggressively and inappropriately than he would be if he understood the source of his bad "mood."

You can help the children you teach or counsel deal more effectively with anger and conflict by bolstering their understanding of themselves, their understanding of others, and their feelings of self-confidence. You can deliver this help by systematically addressing three areas of social-emotional growth:

1. Self-Awareness: Help children identify and talk about their feelings, thoughts and behaviors, and understand the feelings, thoughts, and behaviors of others.

2. Social Interaction: Teach and model effective communication skills, such as active listening and I-statements. Help students become aware of their nonverbal behaviors, and insist that they treat one another with respect and courtesy.

3. Mastery: Give students many opportunities to practice communication and problem-solving skills and reinforce every increment of progress. Don't use your authority to settle their conflicts for them. Help them develop the self-confidence to deal effectively with the people and events in their lives.

Helping children to grow in these three areas greatly increases their resiliency and their ability to manage anger and conflict in creative and positive ways. The next few paragraphs deal with Awareness, Social Interaction and Mastery in greater depth.

Anger, Conflict and Awareness

Aware children know how they feel and what they think. They also know how they are behaving. Although they are conscious of themselves, they aren't self-conscious, insecure, or embarrassed. Their awareness doesn't produce anxiety and they can accept and acknowledge how they really feel, think, and behave.

Aware children are usually capable of resolving conflict and managing anger in ways beneficial to themselves and others. Because they are aware of their own needs, they tend to have rational ways of dealing with anger situations and are less impulsive.

When children lack self-awareness, they are more likely to say and do things that cause conflict and anger in others. They don't realize how their verbal and nonverbal behaviors come across to others. They are equally unaware of the effects of others'

verbal and nonverbal behaviors on them.

The following stories illustrate just how easily conflict can arise in the absence of awareness, both within an individual student and in the same student's ability to respond appropriately to other people.

Mike is frustrated and angry because his parents won't let him go to the game after school with his friends. So all day, he mopes, and scowls, and mutters at his teachers and classmates, until finally someone confronts him and a fight starts.

Jenny, trying to be clever, makes a sarcastic remark while Lisa is giving her oral report. The snide comment embarrasses Lisa and she loses her place. By the time she gets back on track, she is furious at Jenny. During recess, she tells Jenny that they are no longer friends. Jenny is baffled. Completely unaware of her negative verbal style, she thinks Lisa's reaction is extreme and unreasonable.

The basketball coach walks into the YMCA gym one day to find Dave and Joey fighting. He intervenes. When the other kids insist that Dave started the fight, the coach takes Dave into his office for a talk. Dave admits he clobbered Joey when, for the dozenth time, Joey deliberately pushed Dave during a game. Instead of dealing with Joey's pushing the first time, Dave tried to ignore the problem. He was not aware that his resentment and irritation had been building — until he exploded.

Anger, Conflict and Social Interaction

Children with good social skills have a developing awareness of how other people think, feel, and behave. They know how to listen and are pretty good at making themselves understood. They are aware that differences and similarities exist between people, and they understand how one person's behavior causes reactions in others. They are tolerant, recognizing and accepting individual differences between people, without having to yield to their influence.

Anger builds up and conflict often results when a child misreads the verbal and nonverbal behaviors of others, is intolerant of others, or is unable to deal with their intolerance. Poor communicators are easily misunderstood, and frequently instigate anger or conflict unknowingly, just by the things they say. Children who don't listen either fail to hear or misinterpret instructions, requests, and information. Finally, negative peer pressure, or a strong need for peer acceptance, can lead children to do things they would not otherwise do.

The following are examples of how anger arises and conflict can occur when a child lacks social competencies, or comes in contact with someone else who lacks them:

Rose observes two of her classmates standing at the bulletin board, looking at one of her drawings. They are pointing to different parts of the drawing and it seems to Rose that they are making fun of it. So in retaliation, *Rose walks by and "accidentally" pushes one of the girls. After breaking up the ensuing fight, Rose's teacher recalls several instances when Rose has mistaken the behavior of others and reacted with tears, tattling, and accusations.*

Alice and Tim are fourth grade classmates who have been assigned to work on a science project together. One morning the teacher is forced to break up an argument between the two. He asks both children to explain their side of the conflict. Alice, whose science skills are much stronger than Tim's, says that Tim is slow and lazy and that she is tired of doing most of the work. Tim says that Alice rushes ahead and won't give him time to figure out the hard stuff. And she refuses to help him.

Roberto has walked home several times with the new kid, Vince. He likes Vince. However, today Roberto is standing outside the classroom talking with some of the other guys when Vince walks up. One of the guys says something snide about Vince under his breath and the others laugh. So when Vince says hello, Roberto looks away and ignores him. After school, Vince glares at Roberto and heads down the street without him. Roberto feels awful.

Anger, Conflict and Mastery

Children who have achieved a reasonable degree of mastery are self-confident and are willing, even eager, to try new things. They accept challenges, and exhibit a natural, uninhibited enthusiasm. Mastery grows as skills and competencies build. Self-esteem is strengthened when the child recognizes this growth. Self-esteem cannot be overlaid like a facade over weak skills and competencies.

Sometimes conflict occurs because children don't recognize their own abilities. When children underestimate their ability, others sometimes become impatient and angry. When these children fail to achieve, it's not because they can't do something but because fear and insecurity cloud their judgment. Other children overestimate their ability and fail to live up to promises. This, too, causes conflict. Lack of confidence can also cause a child to overcompensate by engaging in behaviors that are socially inappropriate or unacceptable.

A "time bomb" is being carried by any child who always has to be "right" or "best" or "number one" at the expense of others. The frantic drive to be number one is closely related to the child's development of genuine mastery and self-esteem. By the same token, teasing can be a way of being more important by making others seem smaller or less significant. Ruthless competition can cause a child to ride roughshod over the rights of others. Cheating to get better grades, hoarding possessions and cliquishness also cause conflict and can result from a child's search for short cuts to mastery.

The following are examples of how problems can occur when a child lacks mastery or when a child comes in contact with another person whose mastery in certain areas is low.

Jeff loves to swim and spends a great deal of time at the pool. He has been trying very hard lately to master jumping off the board and does okay when no one is watching. Today, just as he is about to jump, five other kids show up and get in line to use the board. Jeff freezes and then begins to shake. Finally, he sits down and slides off the board into the pool. When the other kids laugh, Jeff gets angry and starts splashing water on them.

Ella's class is organizing a mini-carnival to raise money for a field trip. With great bravura, Ella announces that she is going to write an article as well as design an ad for the school paper, and that her contributions will surely double attendance at the carnival. Ella is cautioned that both the article and the ad must be ready by Friday afternoon, but she doesn't flinch. However, between homework, baby-sitting, and numerous other activities, Ella finds no time and she misses the deadline. When Ella's classmates express disappointment, she is quick with excuses.

Kelli and Manuela are having a serious yelling match. Kelli accuses Manuela of hoarding a book from the library. Both girls say they need the book for a class assignment, and the teacher has suggested they work together or take turns using the book at school. Now Manuela has taken the book home and keeps "forgetting" to bring it back. The assignment is due in two days and it is clear that Manuela is setting the stage to receive the highest grade.

When Jesse misses a free throw in basketball, Harold is there, in his usual way, to make fun of the mistake. His low "Missed it, Jesse...heh, heh..." finally hits target. Jesse grabs Harold by the collar and shoves him across the court, hissing, "When you learn to make a basket yourself, shrimpface, you can laugh at me. Until then, shut up!"

Conflict Management Strategies

You will find that children are already using many creative strategies in dealing with conflict. They negotiate, take turns, flip coins, compromise, and use many other methods, all on their own.

You will also find that children need help in building their own positive experiences into an effective system of conflict and anger management. They require help in sorting out positive and negative strategies. They benefit from trying out new ideas, and they need reinforcement when they discover and use creative ways of handling conflict and anger.

The conflict management strategies listed on the next page are simply that, a list, until they have been internalized by the students. To be truly useful and instantly available, the strategies must become the "property" of the child. One of the primary goals of this curriculum guide is to help the child discover workable strategies and practice them until they are his or her own. Use of the Sharing Circle and role-play topics and the group activities will speed the process.

Conflict and Role Playing

Everything in this curriculum guide is preparatory to role playing. Role playing is the "secret sauce" that brings all the strategies together and makes them palatable and easy to assimilate. It is a powerful enzyme in anger and conflict management.

The experiences inherent in the role-play process have their own rewards. Students gain a great deal from being spontaneous, expressing their feelings and ideas, and interacting with one another. Learning becomes personally meaningful and enjoyable.

Conflict Management Strategies

- **Listen carefully to the other person.**

    Let the other person explain his or her side of the story. Pay close attention and try to understand the person's point of view.

- **Explain your position without blaming the other person.**

    Tell your side of the story and express your feelings in a non-threatening way. Use I-statements such as "I feel angry" or "I'm upset" instead of saying, "You made me mad." Using I-statements makes it easier for the other person to listen to you.

- **Allow time to cool off.**

    If either of you is extremely angry, tired, or "out-of-control, " it may be better to agree on a later time to deal with the problem. Allowing a cooling off time for one or both of you may prevent a bigger conflict.

- **Problem solve together to create a "win-win" situation.**

    Make it your goal to find a resolution that both of you can accept. This is best done when both of you are calm enough to consider the other's point of view. You may need to try one or more other strategies first, such as apologizing or listening carefully to the other person's side of the story. Problem solving may also lead to compromise.

- **Be willing to compromise.**

    Both persons in a conflict must cooperate in order to reach a compromise. You will probably have to give up something, but you will get something, too. Use problem solving to reach a compromise both of you can agree on.

- **Say you're sorry.**

    If you're responsible for the conflict, say, "I'm sorry, I didn't mean to do it," or "I'm sorry we got into this fight." Saying, "I'm sorry," doesn't necessarily mean that you are admitting any wrongdoing. "I'm sorry" can just be a way of saying, "I know you are hurt and angry and I feel bad about that." A problem often gets worse when one person feels badly and thinks the other person doesn't care — or care enough. This feeling can be eased by a simple "I'm sorry."

- **Use humor.**

    Making light of a conflict, without making fun of the other person, may ease the tension both of you feel. Humor generally works best when you direct it toward yourself in a natural, lighthearted way. This may help the other person realize that the situation isn't as bad as it seems.

- **Ask for help.**

    When no one can suggest a solution, it's best to ask someone else to step in and help resolve the conflict. The new person can bring new ideas and a fresh perspective to the problem.

- **Know when to walk away.**

    If you find yourself in a situation where you might be physically hurt, walk or run away. If you think the other person might become violent, it's best to say you're sorry and leave quickly rather than try to save face or be tough.

More significantly, role play can be used to promote specific educational outcomes. In this curriculum guide, we have used role play's compelling functions to help students:

- accept the reality and regular occurrence of anger and conflict.
- recognize that experiencing anger and conflict is a normal part of living, playing, and working with others.
- use specific strategies of self-control and anger management.
- apply both logic and creativity to resolving specific conflicts.
- rehearse the language and behaviors inherent in peaceful, cooperative living.
- learn and practice specific strategies for resolving conflicts.

What Is Role Playing?

Role playing, in its simplest sense, is the spontaneous practice of character roles. The students assume the roles in order to actually see and feel the dynamics of a specific situation, and to practice the behaviors required to accomplish their objectives in that situation. It's through this repeated practice that the pro-social skills of conflict resolution become internalized. In this curriculum guide, role plays are used to discover the dynamics of conflict situations, and the overriding objective is always to settle the conflict cooperatively and productively.

Role play is an important group guidance procedure. It is a social-interaction learning device, a group problem-solving method involving discussion, problem analysis, idea generation and testing, observation, evaluation, and decision making. It involves:

1. initial taking of roles;
2. observer reactions to the enactments (discussion);
3. exploration of alternatives through further enactments and discussion;
4. drawing of conclusions, or, generalization and decision making.

Role playing offers the opportunity to explore, through spontaneous enactment and carefully guided discussion, typical anger and conflict provoking situations. In the process, students are helped to become sensitive to the feelings of the people involved, recognize the consequences of the choices they make, and explore the kinds of behaviors that are effective and socially acceptable. They are guided to become sensitive to feelings, and to the consequences of the choices they make, both for themselves and for other people. Through repeated discussion and role plays of specific anger and conflict incidents (many generated by the discussion and role-play topics starting on page 104), students practice a variety of approaches to managing anger and resolving conflict. Gradually they develop skills that enable them to interact more effectively in *all* situations.

Perhaps the most important aspect of the role-playing process is the fact that the students, with the help of their peers, gradually become conscious of the choices they typically make in conflict situations, evaluate the effectiveness of those choices, and begin to replace ineffective behaviors with effective ones.

The Sharing Circle and Role-Play Process—How It's Done

Role playing, as presented here, is actually a combination of a Sharing Circle and role play. First, during the Sharing Circle, in response to the topic presented by the leader, the students share a variety of ideas and experiences related to anger or conflict. Next, they choose one of those experiences to role-play and brainstorm alternative endings to the chosen experience, and role-play at least one positive alternative. Step by step, the process goes like this:

1. Rules are established to guide the Sharing Circle. These rules exist to safeguard both the process and the participants. They are:

- Everyone gets a turn to share, including the leader.
- You can skip your turn if you wish.
- Listen to the person who is sharing.
- There are no interruptions, probing, put-downs, or gossip.
- The time is shared equally.

2. A Sharing Circle topic is announced. The leader states the topic and clarifies its meaning with a brief explanation and two or three examples. The Sharing Circle topics presented in this guide are designed to help the students think about conflict from a variety of vantage points.

3. The Sharing Circle is facilitated by the leader. Students are invited to share their experiences relative to the stated topic. The leader may choose to share an experience, too. The Sharing Circle does not need to take a great deal of time. Depending on the age and number in a group, 10 to 15 minutes should be enough time..

4. The students choose one incident to role play. The student whose incident is chosen retells the story so that everyone has a clear picture of what occurred and the roles of the people involved.

5. The incident is dramatized up to the point of conflict. By coaching and encouraging the actors, the leader helps students understand the feelings, thoughts, and motivations of the various characters and the reasons for the conflict.

6. The students brainstorm alternative resolutions. The students are reminded of the nine "Conflict Management Strategies" presented earlier, and are encouraged to think of other strategies as well. List suggestions on the board.

7. The students choose and role play one positive alternative from the list. The actors reenact the same scenario from the beginning, this time dramatizing the positive conflict resolution chosen by the group. The rest of the group observes carefully.

8. The students evaluate the effectiveness of the resolution. After the role-play, the group talks about whether or not the new ending worked. If it did not work, a second alternative ending is chosen and dramatized.

9. The students discuss the experience and what they learned. This cognitive conclusion helps the students internalize the concepts explored and insights gained through the Sharing Circle and role-play process.

Your Role as Leader

Underlying successful guidance of role playing is a set of basic assumptions about human behavior and the teaching-learning process. Most important is the belief that each student is growing and developing in his or her ability to cope with life situations, including anger and conflicts.

Assuming that the great majority of students have the capacity (if not the skills) to solve their own problems, giving them safe opportunities to make their own decisions allows them to evaluate those decisions and learn from their mistakes. As a leader, this will sometimes mean going along with very low-level attempts to resolve conflicts, not dictating the "best" alternatives, but rather, patiently guiding enactments and discussions so that the students make their own discoveries and gradually move to higher levels of decision-making because of their increased awareness of alternatives.

Another basic assumption in role playing conflict situations is that the alternative behaviors which are enacted are more or less effective depending on their consequences. If you help the students focus on the likely consequences of choosing one course of action over another, you probably will not have to impose your own judgments on their ideas. By carefully questioning and guiding the actors and observers ("How did you feel when Sharon said that?" "Are you completely satisfied with this solution?") you can help them make sound judgments on their own.

The behaviors that students habitually fall back on in conflict situations will probably not change until they develop greater insight into the real effects of those behaviors and the fact that they have other choices. Individuals often know intellectually what is "right" but act on feelings or past behavior patterns. Role playing helps students cope with the reality of their choices, which has far greater impact than merely responding to the verbal judgments of authority figures.

Your job in leading the Sharing Circle and role-play process is to act as a facilitator, giving the students enough latitude to become creatively involved in depicting the situation and resolving the conflict, yet always maintaining sufficient control to keep the dramatization meaningful and on target.

Casting the Role Play:

In an interpersonal conflict situation, there are always at least two roles.

After the child whose conflict is chosen briefly retells the story to clarify the incident and the roles, invite that child to play him or herself — but don't insist. Suppose that Shiela's conflict is chosen and she agrees to play herself. Name the remaining roles one at a time and ask for volunteers to fill them. Allow Shiela to do the selecting. If you think that Shiela is apt to favor her friends, if someone volunteers who has not participated much in the past, or if you think a particular volunteer is uniquely suited to one of the roles, by all means make your suggestion and urge Shiela to follow it. If Shiela does not want to play herself, help her choose someone for the "starring" role as well.

Setting the Stage:

Before beginning the enactment, work with the actors to very briefly plan what they are going to do. Remember that the child whose role play was chosen already retold the story, so outlining the action takes only seconds. For example, "Shiela is standing here, in her front yard. There's the sidewalk, and Rudy, playing her neighbor, comes rushing over from next door. He looks upset."

Encourage Shiela to be the director as well as the leading actor. Give her every opportunity to set the stage herself, while you assist and clarify.

Preparing the Audience:

In the Sharing Circle and role-play process, the conflict incident is role played at least twice. The first time, it is role played up to the point of conflict. Then the action is stopped and the nature of the problem is clarified so that the group can brainstorm strategies for resolving the conflict. The second time, the role play commences again at the beginning and is role played up to the point of conflict; however, this time the chosen pro-social resolution is inserted into the scenario and acted out as a way of testing its effectiveness.

The audience has two tasks. During the initial role play, instruct the observers to watch and listen very carefully, trying their best to understand the feelings and ideas of each of the characters. Urge them to place themselves in each person's position in order to look at the situation with that person and see what he or she sees. Explain that the observers have to understand each character's viewpoint before they can decide whether they agree or disagree with that person and before they can think of alternative solutions that will help that person. Remind them that they will be trying to come up with a win-win resolution.

During the second role play, instruct the audience to again listen carefully and try to think and feel as though inside each character, but this time with the objective of evaluating the chosen resolution. Remind them that they will be asked to judge to what extent the resolution meets the needs of each character.

Guiding the Role Play:

These are not elaborate dramatizations, so very little if any intervention is ever necessary. If a player forgets to pick up the action at the appropriate time, give the person a quick nonverbal cue. If someone gets stuck, ask, "How do you feel in your role right now?" or "Show us what your character would do or say."

Discussion and Evaluation:

The discussion that follows a role play is one of the most vital phases of the process. While the taking of roles allows students to experience the perspectives of the various people in a conflict, it is in the give and take of discussion that problem solving procedures are refined and learned.

Through the discussion, students learn the consequences of their choices. Comments like, "If I said that to my neighbor, he'd be on the phone to my mom in a second!" or "If I were your neighbor, I'd want you to help me clean up the mess" give the student direct and immediate feedback about specific behaviors and alternative strategies.

Your role is to guide the discussion by asking stimulating open-ended questions. Prompts may be needed before and during the brainstorming process ("What will solve this problem?" "Think about how each person feels." "Can you think of a strategy that will resolve the situation for both people?") and at the conclusion of the role play ("How well did our solution work?" "Do you think this conflict is completely settled?" "Who came out ahead with this resolution?" "Were there any losers with this strategy?"). These questions have two objectives: 1) to continue clarifying the nature of the conflict and the positions of the parties involved, and 2) to evaluate the selected resolution.

The final discussion — and it needn't be lengthy — should focus on *overall learnings*. Ask questions like, "What did you learn from this activity?" "How will this experience help you if you have a conflict like this in *your* life?" or "How can a conflict like this be prevented from happening in the first place?"

Reenactments:

There are two reasons to reenact a conflict: to get a better result and/or to compare the consequences of different strategies. If a strategy is ineffective or makes the situation worse, ask the group to pick a second strategy from the list of alternatives. Role play and evaluate the second one just as you did the first.

If the person whose conflict was dramatized would like to compare different approaches, or if you think the role play lends itself particularly well to comparative evaluation, role play two or three different strategies. Gear your final discussion to the relative merits and consequences of the different resolutions.

Watching the Clock:

After reading through the process, the steps involved, and the leadership

responsibilities, you may be thinking
that the Sharing Circle and role-play
process is both involved and time
consuming. Actually, the process
is not nearly as time intensive as
it might appear. *Describing* and
reading about it takes time because
distinctions must be made between
the back-and-forth shifts from
Sharing Circle to role play. In reality,
each phase moves quickly and the
entire process is over in just a few
minutes.

Remember that you can always
return to a particular role play during
subsequent sessions, for reenactments
(to try different alternatives) and
for further discussion. However,
be prepared for time warps and
sessions that vanish in a flash. The
enthusiasm and involvement of the
group may very well banish time from
everyone's consciousness. Enjoy the
process!

Group Activities

Identifying Feelings
An Activity for Young Children

Objective:

The children will:

— develop awareness of their own feelings, both positive and negative.

— be able to accept and talk about their feelings.

Materials:

space dividers (chalk, chairs, tape, cardboard boxes, etc.)

Directions:

Pick two areas in the room that are physically separated. Designate one area as "The Happy Face Place," and the other area as "The Sad Face Place." Mark these areas. (See materials list.)

Introduce this activity by telling the children: *I want you to think about feelings-happy ones and sad ones. I'm going to say some things to you. When one of these things makes you feel happy, go to the 'Happy Face Place' (point out the location).*

When one of these things makes you feel sad, go to the 'Sad Face Place' (point out the location). In the 'Happy Face Place' we will make happy faces. In the 'Sad Face Place' we will make sad faces.

Read each of the following statements. Allow enough time so that the children feel comfortable in making their choices.

Face Place Feelings

a. You fall down and skin your knee.

b. Your friend doesn't want to play with you today.

c. Your mother gives you two helpings of ice cream.

d. A little puppy wants to play with you.

e. Somebody sticks their tongue out at you.

f. Your teacher reads your favorite story.

g. You get lost in the supermarket.

h. It's raining and you can't go outside to play.

i. You make a brand new friend.

j. You break your father's favorite-dish.

k. You go for a long ride in the car.

l. Your shoes are too tight.

m. You get to stay up late one night.

n. You learn you're going to the zoo.

o. It's your birthday.

p. Someone steps on your toe.

q. You tear a page in your friend's book.

r. You accidentally bump into someone and he or she yells at you.

s. You see two people having a fight.

At the conclusion, use the following prompts and questions to encourage discussion.

Discussion Questions:

1. Think of a time when you had a happy feeling. Tell us about it.

2. Think of a time when you had a sad feeling, and tell us about it.

3. Does everyone have these feelings?

4. Are sad and happy feelings equally important?

5. What are all the different ways you can show that you are happy?

6. What are all the different ways you can show that you are sad.

Variation:

Ask the children to draw pictures of things that make them happy and sad-one paper for happy things, the other for sad things.

Using Puppets to Express Feelings
An Activity for Young Children

Objectives:

The children will:

— get in touch with and express their own feelings.

— test out new methods of handling conflict in a safe and threat-free atmosphere.

Materials:

a puppet for each child; puppet stage

(See page 23 for puppet and stage directions.)

Directions:

Gather the children into a circle and provide a puppet to each child. From the following list, give them ideas to try out with their puppets. Allow time between each statement so that they may get "involved" in each emotion. Encourage their efforts. Try to get all the children participating.

a. Have your puppets be happy. How can you show your puppets are happy?

b. Have your puppets be sad. How can you show they are sad?

c. Have your puppets be angry. How can you show they are angry?

d. Have your puppets be surprised. How can you show they are surprised?

e. Have your puppets be tired. How can you show they are tired?

f. Have your puppets be excited. How can you show they are excited?

After these warm-up exercises, ask two of the children to come to the puppet stage and act out play#1 from the list of "Conflict Plays".

Read the sentence describing play #1 and ask the children to act it out with their puppets. Allow two to three minutes.

Once this first play has been acted out, ask the whole group to think

about how the conflict can be handled
in a positive way. As a group, decide
one of the suggested resolutions to the
conflict, and ask the children to act it
out with their puppets.

Repeat the three-step process for each
play. First, two children act out the
conflict as written; second, the entire
group brainstorms how the conflict
can be resolved in a positive fashion;
and third, one resolution is chosen
and acted out by the two children.

Conflict Plays

Play 1
> A child loses a book. Another child finds it. Both say the book is theirs. An argument begins.

Play 2
> Two children reach the same toy at the same time. Both children want to play with it and they argue over it.

Play 3
> One child has let another borrow a toy. The second child lost the toy and the first child is angry. They are arguing.

Play 4
> A child is late for a favorite TV show and goes running into the house, knocking over a younger brother. An argument starts.

Play 5
> A brother and sister want to watch different TV programs. They get into a fight about which one to watch.

Play 6
> A child hits another child with a ball and thinks it's very funny. The second child gets mad because it hurt. They get into an argument.

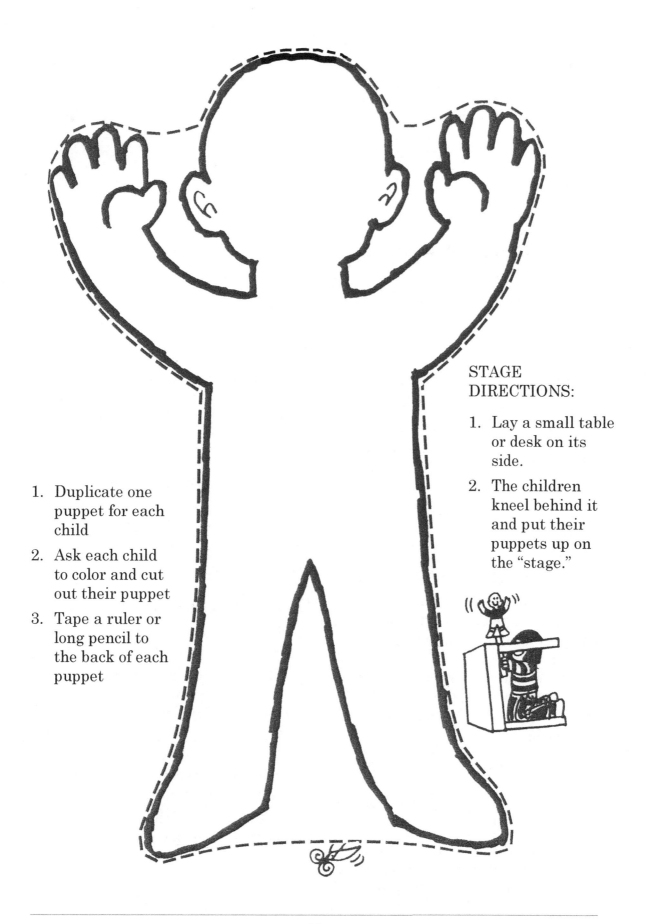

1. Duplicate one puppet for each child

2. Ask each child to color and cut out their puppet

3. Tape a ruler or long pencil to the back of each puppet

STAGE DIRECTIONS:

1. Lay a small table or desk on its side.

2. The children kneel behind it and put their puppets up on the "stage."

Positive Endings
An Activity for Young Children

Objective:

The children will identify positive alternatives to conflict in a non-threatening environment

Materials:

the story cards, duplicated and cut-out from the next three pages

Directions:

Work with small groups for this activity.

Tell the children that you are going to show them some pictures that depict a conflict or disagreement taking place between two children. Then you will show them some pictures that will give ideas on how the conflict can be handled. They will choose which idea they like best.

Present one story at a time by reading and showing the first three frames. Then present the three frames depicting possible alternatives.

Tell the children that there are several things that could be done, but you would like them to decide on one "alternative."

Explain alternative by saying: *Alternatives are different ways of doing something. In this case the alternatives are the different ways these problems or conflicts can be solved.*

Read all three alternative frames for each story. Let the children decide which alternative they like best, and place that frame at the end of the story.

After each story is finished, ask the following questions:

Discussion Questions:

1. Have you ever solved a conflict using that alternative?

2. If the children in the story don't resolve their problem, what do you think will happen? How would they feel?

3. How do you think they will feel if they handle the problem using the alternative you have picked?

Leave the cards for the children to play with at their leisure.

1.

3. conflict

alternative

sharing

alternative

taking turns

altnerative

fighting

26

Danny's Big Game
An Activity for Young Children

Objectives:

The children will:

— state that conflicts can occur when a person promises to do something and overestimates his or her ability to carry through.

— identify how such behavior can cause trouble.

Materials:

assorted art materials

Directions:

Read the story, "Danny's Big Game," aloud to the children.

After the story, ask these and other of your own questions to generate discussion.

Discussion Questions:

1. If you were Danny, what do you think you would have done? Would you try to bring all the equipment back by yourself? Would you let someone help you carry the equipment?

2. Have you ever tried to do something all by yourself and it didn't work out? How did you feel?

3. Have you ever tried to do something all by yourself and it did work out? How did you feel?

Extension:

Ask the children to draw a picture about a time they tried to do something all by themselves. If they are able to write have them write a story about it also.

Ask the children to read their stories or tell about their pictures.

DANNY'S BIG GAME

Danny has wanted to play baseball with his older brother Ricky and his baseball team for a long time. And one day, one of the members of the team was home in bed with a sore throat and the team needed someone to take his place.

"I'll play!" shouted Danny. "I'm good now. I've been really practicing hard for a long time. Please let me!" Ricky and the other children on the team talked about it for a while and finally they told Danny he could play with them but that he'd have to go to the house of the sick boy and get the equipment he had which was needed for the game.

"I'd better go with you, Danny. I don't think you can carry the bases, bats, balls and everything all by yourself," Ricky told Danny.

Danny was afraid that the other kids would think he was too little to do all that by himself, so he straightened his shoulders and said, "Hey, I can carry everything. I don't need any help." and off he rushed.

About a half hour later, Danny came trudging back to the field, loaded down with bases, bats and gloves. Danny had a triumphant smile on his face as the other children helped to unload him.

Then Ricky let out a yell: "Hey, Danny! Where's the ball? It's not here."

Danny's big smile turned to a confused look. "I thought I had it when I started out," he told everyone. But they couldn't find it and the game had to be delayed, which made everyone grumpy. Danny got so grumpy he didn't play well. He felt he wouldn't get another chance to play for a long time, and he was sorry he had tried to do everything himself. If someone else had helped him, he probably wouldn't have lost the ball and the game would have gone much better.

How Was Joey Feeling?
An Activity for Young Children

Objective:

The children will:

— identify feelings associated with performance and conflict.

— describe the relationship between events and emotional reactions.

Materials:

cut out figures from page 32; drawing materials

Directions:

Read "Joey and the Diving Board", using the cut out figures to illustrate the story. These figures are put up one at a time as the story progresses. The appropriate place to introduce each figure is marked in brackets in the story.

After reading the story, ask the following questions or others you may think of.

Discussion Questions:

1. How was Joey feeling when he first got up on the diving board?

2. How was Joey feeling when he finally left the pool?

3. When Joey got too scared to jump and he started yelling at the other kids, what else do you think he could have done?

4. If he had done something else, do you think he would have felt better afterwards?

5. Have you ever really wanted to do something but you just couldn't seem to get the confidence to do it? How did that make you feel?

6. Have you ever wanted to do something that scared you a little, but you tried anyway and you did it? How did that make you feel?

Extension:

Ask the children to draw a picture of a time when they did something they really wanted to do.

JOEY AND THE DIVING BOARD

(Put up diving board.)

Joey is a pretty good swimmer and he wants to jump off the diving board. He has already done it twice when his dad was sitting on the side of the pool. He thought he would try it again today.

(Put Joey up at beginning of board.)

When Joey got to the pool, there was hardly anyone there. He looked around, then slowly walked out onto the long board. He was a little scared.

(Put Joey at end of board.)

When he got to the end and looked down, it seemed as though the water was deeper than usual. His knees started to shake, but he still wanted to jump. He could feel his heart making thumps and his toes felt tingly and so did the ends of his fingers.

(Put the group of kids up.)

He was all ready to jump, when he heard voices behind him. He turned around. A group of kids had just arrived and were waiting to use the board. That made him really scared. They were all talking and laughing among themselves and that made him imagine they were all watching him and making fun of how scared he was.

When Joey looked down into the water again, it looked even deeper this time.

(Put coach up.)

Just then the coach came out and yelled, "C'mon, Joey! The other kids want to use the board, too!" This made Joey so frightened and upset he knew he couldn't jump. He had to turn around and walk off. He felt really bad about himself, and wished he wasn't so scared about jumping off the board. He really didn't know what to do about his bad feelings so he started yelling at the other kids:

> "I really didn't want to jump into the dumb old pool anyway! That's no fun. You guys can be stupid and jump if you want but I'm not!"

When he said these things to the other kids they started to yell back and call him chicken.

Joey just felt really bad so he got his clothes and left the pool.

Cut figures out
and use with
the story Joey
and the Diving
Board

Learning to Work Together
Cooperative Enterprises

Objectives:

The students will:

— collaborate with peers to complete an assigned task.

— discuss how the lack of cooperation contributes to conflict.

— describe cooperative behaviors involved in working with others.

Materials:

depending on the specific project, drawing or writing materials; puzzles; trash/scrap items, string, glue and other fasteners

Directions:

Cooperation and collaboration are important skills for children to develop. Many childhood conflicts occur because children don't cooperate and work well together. This activity provides a venue for looking specifically at issues of inclusion, interdependency, cooperation, and collaboration.

Have the students form pairs, triads, or small groups. Give them an assignment from the list below that requires collaboration:

• Have the students produce a drawing that illustrates a feeling, such as anger, sadness, confusion, worry, compassion, or joy.

• Have them write a short poem about a feeling, and illustrate it.

• Provide a variety of small trash items, scraps, and recyclables, and have the students create a sculpture, collage, or some other product.

• Give the students a topic and ask them to collaborate in writing a short story.

• In circles of six or eight, have students participate in group story telling, by going around the circle and taking turns adding sentences.

- Have the students put together a puzzle or solve a design problem, such as the creation of a mechanism for raising school awareness about peaceful conflict resolution.

Require that the groups demonstrate inclusion[1] and interdependence[2] as they work together, giving equal time to every member and not allowing anyone to dominate the process.

Have the groups show and/or display their final products for everyone to see. Facilitate a culminating discussion.

Discussion Questions:

1. What was it like to work together on this project?

2. How did you make sure that everyone had an equal chance to participate?

3. Did angry moments happen or did you experience any conflicts? If so, how did you resolve them?

4. What can you do if you think someone in the group is dominating the process — not letting you be a leader or share your ideas?

5. What can you do if your partner stands back and lets you do all the work?

[1] Inclusion: The action of including or of being included within a group or structure

[2] Interdependence: Two or more people being dependent upon each other.

Donor Dollars
A Group Decision-Making Activity

Objectives:

The students will:

— experience group conflict caused by opposing opinions and beliefs.

— use communication and negotiation skills to reach a group decision.

Materials:

one copy of the list of choices for each small group; whiteboard

Directions:

Have the students form small groups of four to six. Announce that the members of each group are going to work together to make a decision. In your own words, elaborate:

I want you to pretend that you are the student council for our school. This is an exciting time for you because you have an important decision to make. The council has been given $10,000 by an anonymous donor, which you must decide how to spend. However, the donor has narrowed your range of choices. You must decide from among six alternatives.

Give each group a copy of the list of choices. Read through the list with the students:

1. Take the student council (your group) to Disney World

2. Donate the money to a local children's hospital to be used to fund a child's organ transplant.

3. Host a big party for the entire school.

4. Donate the money to a homeless shelter.

5. Fund badly needed remodeling at a nearby senior center.

6. Give every teacher at your school a cash bonus.

Explain to the students that they will have 20 minutes to reach a decision. List the following rules for interaction on the board and discuss as needed:

- One person speaks at a time, with no interruptions.

- Listen to and consider the ideas and opinions of all members.

- Agree on one choice that is acceptable to all members of the group.

- Consider the benefits and drawbacks of each alternative.

After calling time, give the groups an additional 5 minutes to discuss their behavior during the decision-making process. Then gather the entire group together for a culminating discussion.

Discussion Questions

1. What kind of communication took place in your group?

2. What were the major disagreements or conflicts in your group?

3. What conflict management skills were used to resolve disagreements?

4. Did anyone take the role of mediator in your group? If so, how was that done?

5. What did you learn about conflict management from this activity? What did you learn about group decision making?

Variations:

Have the groups achieve consensus on a first and second choice; on first, second, and third choices; or on a rank ordering of all alternatives.

It Takes Two Hands
Reading, Dramatization, and Discussion

Objectives:

The students will:

— read and perform an allegorical story and explain its meaning.

— identify specific ways in which people need each other.

— explain that a peaceful resolution of anger or conflict requires a coming together of both/all disputants.

Materials:

one copy of the experience sheet, "It Takes Two Hands to Clap," for each student

Directions:

Read to your students the allegorical story, "It Takes Two Hands to Clap." Use one hand to dramatize each line. When you get to the last line, instead of clapping your own two hands together, "discover" the hand of a nearby student and clap your hand against hers.

Next, distribute the experience sheets and ask the students to read along with you, making the appropriate hand motions.

Finally, have the students form pairs, one partner assuming the role of the "reader" and the other the "hand." This approach allows both parts to be fully dramatized. Encourage the readers to put lots of feeling into each line, convincingly conveying the emotions described. Urge the "hands" to use big, exaggerated movements. Have the partners switch roles and do a second reading.

To avoid excessive repetition, have three or four pairs perform in unison for the rest of the group. Conclude with a discussion.

Discussion Questions:

1. What is this story really about? (loneliness, people needing one another, communication, etc.)

2. Why does the hand feel joyful when it finds another hand?

3. How does it feel to discover that
   someone you like enjoys doing the
   same things you do?

4. When two people have a conflict,
   how many does it take to agree on
   a resolution?

5. When you've been in a conflict
   with someone, how does it feel
   to reach a peaceful agreement,
   shake hands, and be friends again?
   Could you do that alone?

It Takes Two Hands to Clap
Experience Sheet

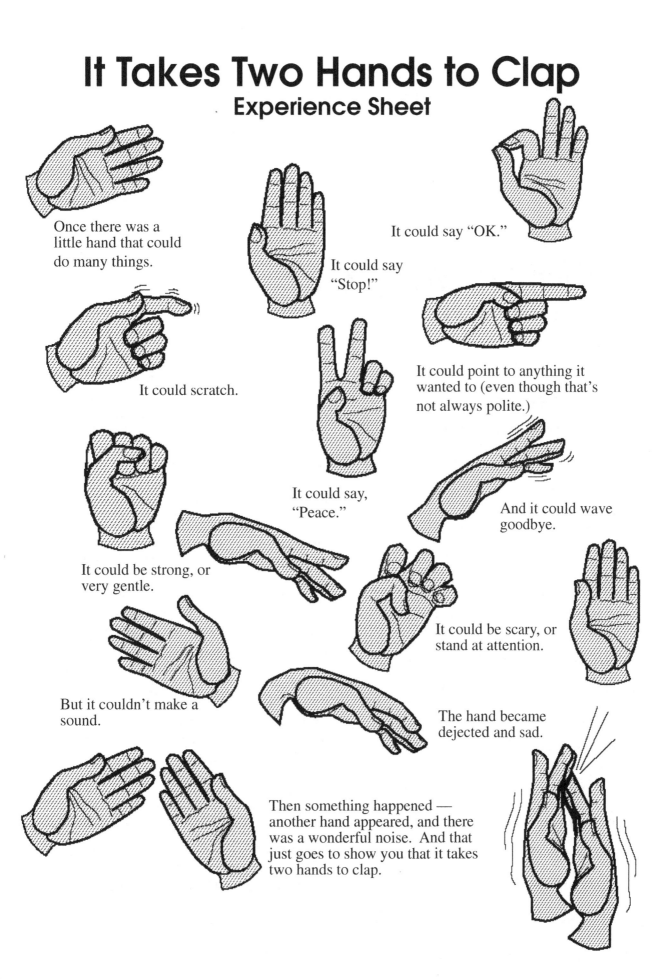

Once there was a little hand that could do many things.

It could say "Stop!"

It could say "OK."

It could scratch.

It could point to anything it wanted to (even though that's not always polite.)

It could say, "Peace."

And it could wave goodbye.

It could be strong, or very gentle.

It could be scary, or stand at attention.

But it couldn't make a sound.

The hand became dejected and sad.

Then something happened — another hand appeared, and there was a wonderful noise. And that just goes to show you that it takes two hands to clap.

What Do You See?
Experiment in Perception

Objectives:

The **students** will:

— recognize that another person's point of view can be as valid as one's own.

— accept the validity of another point of view.

Materials:

writing materials; copies of pictures A, B, and C cut out separately (on page 42) to display to the children

Directions:

This activity uses the familiar drawing that can be perceived either as a vase or as two profiles, depending on which is emphasized. The activity is based on the idea that the picture seen the first time will continue to be the one seen subsequently even when neither is emphasized.

Divide the class in half.

Show picture A to one half.

Show picture B to the other half. It is very important that neither group sees the picture that is shown to the other group.

After both groups have had a few moments to view, remove the pictures. Display picture C for the entire group and have each child write a description of what he or she sees in the picture, without conferring with one another.

Ask volunteers from both groups to take turns reading their descriptions to the whole class.

Laughter may erupt as one group hears the picture described by a member of the other group. While laughter is a normal release, do not allow the students to make derogatory remarks to each other.

After several students have read their descriptions, it will be apparent to everyone that each group has a different opinion about what was seen. Allow free discussion. Each group will probably be sure that it is right and the other is wrong.

After discussion, show the entire group all three pictures and explain that both viewpoints were correct. How they perceived the picture depended on which they saw the first time.

Now, ask the class the following questions and any you can think of:

Discussion Questions:

1. Why did group A think group B was wrong and vice versa?

2. Why was it so hard to see the picture the way the other group saw it?

3. Have you ever had something like this happen to you before (when you thought someone was wrong and you were right, but you were really both right)? Tell us about it.

4. What have you learned from this activity?

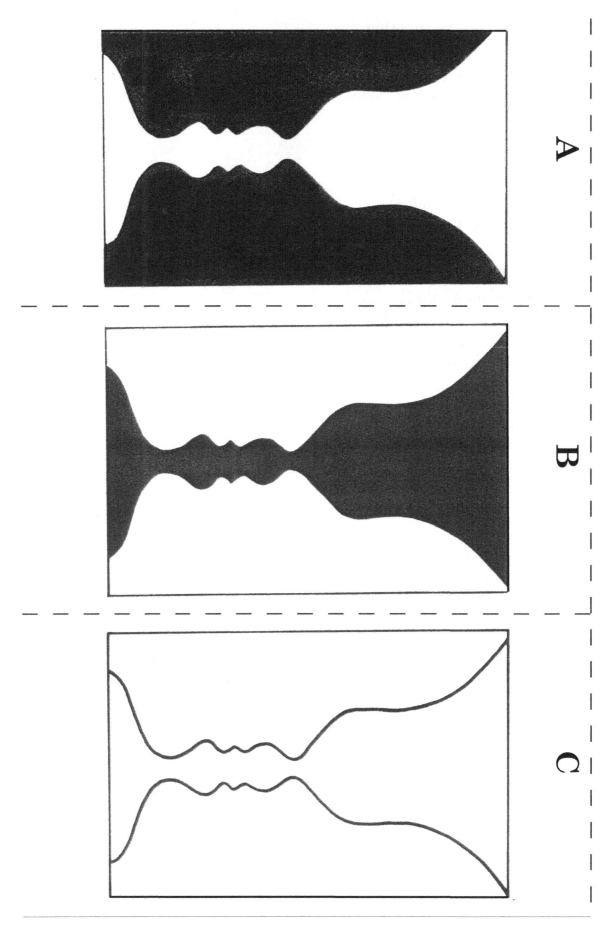

What Makes Good Friends?
Creative Writing and Discussion

Objectives:

The children will:

— understand that relationships with other people are important components in anyone's life.

— become aware of behaviors that they can use to foster positive interactions in their daily lives.

— see how their behaviors can be used to help them manage conflicts more positively.

Materials:

materials for letter writing.

Directions:

Ask the children to write a letter to a friend. Explain that it can be their best friend or someone they just like. It can be someone their age or someone younger or older. It can be an adult.

In writing the letter ask the children to concentrate on the following things:

a. Write about all the things that your friend does that make him or her a good friend.

b. Write about the reasons you like to be with your friend.

c. Write about how your friend treats you and talks to you.

d. Write about a special time you had together and why this time was special.

When the children have finished writing, explain that they may mail or e-mail the letter to their friend if they want, but that the choice is theirs.

Ask volunteers to read their letters aloud to the class.

After all who want to share their letters have done so, ask the following questions.

Discussion Questions

1. What are some of the reasons we like to be with our friends?

2. What are some of the ways our friends treat us and talk to us?

3. How does that make us want to treat our friends in return?

4. What do you think it would be like if everybody treated everyone else like good friends?

I Feel Anger
Experience sheet and Discussion

Objectives:

The students will:

— identify feelings and sensations associated with anger.

— describe how anger makes them feel.

— discuss the importance of controlling anger.

Materials:

one copy of the experience sheet, "Where Do You Feel Anger?" for each student

Directions:

Facilitate a discussion about the feelings and sensations generated by anger. By asking these and other questions:

- *How does your body feel when you are angry?*

- *What happens to your energy level when you are angry? How well are you able to study?*

- *What effect does being angry have on sleep?*

Distribute a copy of the experience sheet, "Where Do You Feel Your Anger", to each student. Go over the directions, and give the students a few minutes to complete it. Conduct a debriefing session. Ask volunteers to share their drawings and describe the feelings and sensations represented. Discuss what the students have observed about anger and what it does to their bodies and minds, reminding students that they have the power to control anger.

Conclude by leading a group discussion using these and additional questions.

Discussion Questions:

1. What kinds of things make you angry?

2. What do you usually do when you are angry?

3. What helps you get over being angry?

4. How does it feel to be around someone who is very angry?

5. Why should people avoid making decisions when they are angry?

Where Do You Feel Your Anger?
Experience Sheet

Directions:

On the outline of the body below draw what happens to you when you are angry. Draw your angry feelings – Use colors and symbols to show where you feel anger and how your body feels when you are angry.

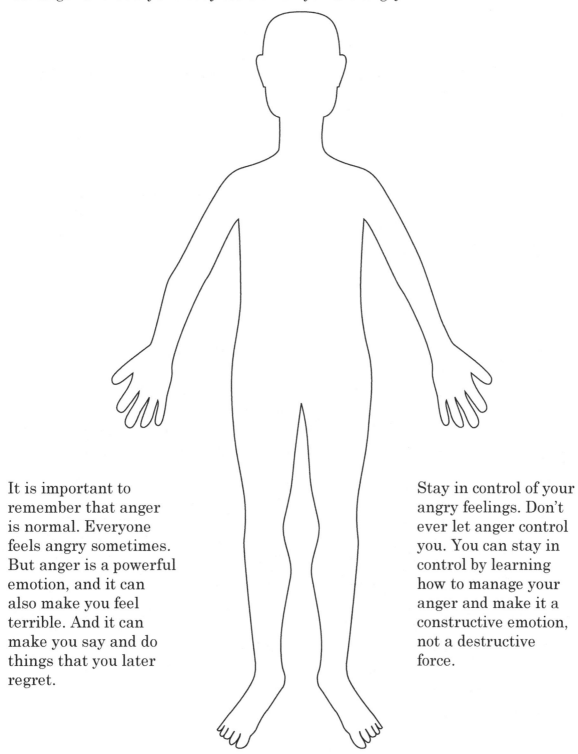

It is important to remember that anger is normal. Everyone feels angry sometimes. But anger is a powerful emotion, and it can also make you feel terrible. And it can make you say and do things that you later regret.

Stay in control of your angry feelings. Don't ever let anger control you. You can stay in control by learning how to manage your anger and make it a constructive emotion, not a destructive force.

Learning to Control My Anger
Experience Sheet and Discussion

Objectives:

The students will:
- — identify people, conditions, and situations that tend to make them angry.
- — describe constructive ways to manage their anger.

Materials:

one copy of the experience sheet, "I Can Control My Anger," for each student

Directions:

Lead the students in a discussion about anger. Acknowledge that it is an uncomfortable emotion that can sometimes be difficult to control. However, emphasizing that it is normal to feel angry at times, and that anger can play a useful role in day-to-day life. Make these additional points:

- Anger is a normal human emotion. It is neither bad nor good.

- Volatile expressions of anger, if they happen often, can negatively affect relationships and can have negative health consequences as well.
- There are healthy and appropriate ways to manage anger.
- It is how we react to a situation, not the situation itself, that causes anger and other emotions.

Ask the students to think of ways they can appropriately express the energy that builds up inside as a result of anger. Write their suggestions on the board and discuss.

Divide the class into groups of three or four. Have the groups brainstorm additional acceptable ways of dealing with anger. Ask each group to share two or three ideas with the class.

Remind the students that if they know what makes them angry, they can learn to recognize the onset of angry feelings and can do something to calm down or cool down.

Distribute the experience sheets and go over the directions. Give the students a few minutes to list situations and conditions that make them angry and ways to manage the anger. When they have finished, ask volunteers to read some of their items to the group.

Elaborate on each example and use it to generate further discussion. Focus less on the situations (and their justification) and more on anger-management strategies.

Discussion Questions:

1. Why is it important to control anger?

2. What are the most common causes of anger in our group?

3. What ideas for controlling anger work best for you?

4. What new ideas for controlling anger would you like to try?

5. What can you do if nothing you try helps to lessen your anger?

6. What happens when people are unable to control their anger?

7. What techniques for reducing anger have worked for you?

8. What happens if you let anger build up inside over hours or days?

I Can Control My Anger
Experience Sheet

Do certain things almost always make you angry? Do you react angrily to the same situations-or the same people-over and over? Maybe you get angry when you don't get your way. Or when your brother or sister uses your things without asking.

In the left column, list things that usually make you angry. In the right column, list things you can do to deal with your angry feelings. .

What Makes Me Angry	What I Can Do
1.	
2.	
3.	
4.	
5.	
6.	
7.	
8.	
9.	
10.	

Thinking About My Anger
Moderating Thoughts to Reduce Anger

Objectives:

The students will:

— demonstrate an understanding of an anger sequence: event—thoughts—feelings.

— practice substituting moderate thoughts for angry thoughts as one way of reducing anger.

Materials:

whiteboard; a copy of the experience sheet, "Anger Sequence," for each student

Directions:

Tell the students that in this activity they will have an opportunity to discover a new way of handling anger. Ask them to consider that angry feelings are not actually caused by situations and events, but rather by the thoughts a person has about those situations and events. Once the thoughts about an event (often extreme) are identified, those thoughts can be replaced with different thoughts (usually more moderate) as one way of controlling anger. Explain to the students that you are going to demonstrate this concept using a chart on the board.

Write four headings across the top of the board:

Event   Thoughts   Feelings
Substitute Thoughts

Under the Event column, write "Mom won't let me go to the dance with my friends." Skip the second column and ask the students what their feelings might be in this situation. The students will probably suggest words such as mad, furious, and miserable. Write several of these words in the Feelings column. Then go back to the Thoughts column, and ask the students what their thoughts might be concerning the same situation. Elicit answers such as these: She's being mean. She doesn't understand how important it is to me. She never wants me to have fun.

Explain to the students that it is not the event, but the thoughts about the event that cause the feelings. Refer to the sentences in the second column and point out that any of these thoughts about the event could create angry feelings. Explain that no situation, event, or person makes us have a particular feeling. Through our thoughts, we choose our feelings, even if we are not aware of it.

Next, suggest that if the thoughts recorded in the second column can be moderated, the feelings too will change. Help the students create new thought statements such as: Mom thinks she is looking out for my safely, She has family plans the night of the dance and wants me to be with the family. There will be more dances this year. Record them in the last column, Substitute Thoughts. Point out that these moderated thoughts will reduce the anger.

Distribute experience sheets.

Under the "Event" heading, ask the students to list three real or hypothetical situations/events in which they are certain they would feel angry. Under the "Thoughts" heading, have them write the thoughts they would have in each situation. Under the "Feelings" heading, ask them to write down the feelings that these thoughts would create. Finally, challenge the students to come up with moderated thoughts that could be substituted for the original thoughts about the situation and to write those under the "Substitute Thoughts" heading.

When all of the students have completed their charts, invite individuals to share one or more of their "anger sequences." After each example, ask the group how their feelings might change as a result of the substitute thoughts. Emphasize that when they find themselves reacting to a situation too strongly, the students can improve their disposition by rethinking the situation. This ability takes practice and perseverance, but it works.

Discussion Questions:

1. Why do we choose to feel angry in certain situations?

2. When you are angry, why is it important to rethink the situation?

3. What is easy about sequencing anger? What is difficult about it?

Anger Sequence
Changing My Thoughts to Reduce Anger

Experience Sheet

Event	Thoughts
1.	1.
2.	2.
3.	3.

Feelings	Substitute Thoughts
1.	1.
2.	2.
3.	3.

How Listening Lowers Anger
Practice Listening Skills

Objectives:

The students will:
- — identify and rehearse active listening behaviors.
- — practice restating the words of another person.

Materials:

whiteboard; writing implements

Directions:

In this activity, the students work in pairs. One partner speaks about a topic. The other listens and restates what he or she hears. The speaker then has an opportunity to give feedback to the listener regarding the quality and accuracy of the listener's restatement.

Tell the students that a good strategy for resolving conflicts or lowering the level of anger is to listen carefully to the other person. Explain that good listening includes 1) hearing what the other person is saying and 2) showing the other person that you are really listening. This is called "active listening." In your own words, explain these benefits of active listening:

By listening carefully to what the other person says, you are able to understand that person's feelings and point of view. By restating what you hear, you not only prove that you are paying attention, you help the other person express feelings and thoughts. You may even help solve a problem. Both speaker and listener gain something when active listening occurs.

Ask the students to help you brainstorm ways in which one person can show another that he or she is really listening. Write all ideas on the board, and discuss how each behavior demonstrates good listening. Elicit responses such as:

- · facing the other person
- · looking into the other person's eyes
- · nodding at appropriate times
- · not allowing yourself to interrupt

- waiting for a pause before asking the other person to clarify a point
- restating what the other person says

Have the students choose partners; then give the following directions:

Decide who is the speaker and who is the listener. Speakers, you will have 2 minutes to talk about a topic which I will announce. Listeners, you will demonstrate active listening behaviors. You will also listen carefully and try to remember everything that is said. When I call "Time" after 2 minutes, listeners will have 1 minute to retell everything they remember hearing. Talk directly to the speaker and include any ideas, details, or specific language that you can remember. Finally, speakers will have 1 minute to correct anything that their listener misunderstood, as well as to describe how it felt to be listened to.

After the first round, have the partners switch roles and repeat the entire process using the same or a different topic. Allow 2 minutes for the speaker to address the topic, 1 minute for the listener to restate what he or she hears, and 1 minute for feedback to the listener by the speaker.

Suggested topics:
- My best school memory
- My worst school memory
- A famous person I would like to meet and why
- If I had a million dollars...
- If I were an animal...
- If I ruled the world...

Conclude the activity by discussing how it feels to be heard and understood. Explain that listening carefully to another person and showing that you are listening can be an effective way to resolve conflict and lower feelings of anger, because what the other person may need most is to have his or her feelings and ideas listened to and accepted.

Discussion Questions:

1. How did you feel when your partner showed that he or she was listening carefully to what you were saying?

2. How did you feel when your partner was able to retell so much of what you said?

3. Why do you think it is important to listen carefully to the other person and show that you are listening?

4. How can listening help resolve a conflict?

Learning to Make I-Statements
Assertive Skill Development

Objectives:

The children will:
- learn how to construct an assertive I-statement.
- compare I-statements to You-statements
- practice the use of I-statements in conflict situations.

Materials:

writing materials for the students; whiteboard or chart paper and markers

Directions:

Tell the students that you want to talk with them about one of the most effective communication tools available to any person who is attempting to resolve a conflict. That tool is called an *I-statement*. In your own words, explain:

I-statements get their name from the fact that they begin with the word,

"I." When you use an I-statement, you are talking about yourself — your perceptions, your beliefs, your feelings, and your wishes.

I-statements are an effective way to talk to people when you are mad at them or frustrated by them. With an I-statement, you express your own concerns. In order to express them, you have to recognize what they are.

When the listener hears an I-statement, the listener knows that she or he has done something that you object to. The listener also knows that you feel badly about the behavior.

By using an I-statement, you can convey a strong message without making the listener feel terrible or incapable.

I-statements are a clear and nonthreatening way to tell people what you want and how you feel.

On the board, write the following I-message formula:

1. *I feel _____ .*
2. *when you _____ .*
3. *because _____ .*

Provide several examples:

"I feel mad when you push in front of me in line, because I am very hungry and don't want to wait any longer to get my lunch."

"I feel worried when you copy my paper, because I'm afraid we'll both get into trouble."

"I feel sad when you say things about me behind my back, because it makes me not trust you anymore."

Ask the students to take out a piece of paper and write down the formula. Have them think back to a recent conflict which they experienced, observed, or helped resolve. Give them a few minutes to write an I-statement expressing the view of each person in the conflict (a total of at least two statements).

When they have finished, go around the group and ask the students to read their I-statements. Coach and correct, as needed, ensuring that all the students grasp the concept and can use the formula. If time permits, role play some of the situations.

To clarify even further, compare I-statements to You-statements. In your own words, explain:

A You-statement is the opposite of an I-statement. It gets its name from the fact that it often begins with the word, "You." For example:
"You jerk, no cuts!"
"You cheater, stop copying my paper."
"You're a two-faced liar! See if I ever tell you anything again!"

You-statements are often blaming and hurtful. When you make a You-statement, the listener may feel criticized, judged, or accused, and may conclude that you think he or she is a bad person. When a You-statement is made, the listener does not think about making a decision to change, but instead thinks about defending himself or herself.

Answer questions and clarify. Facilitate a culminating discussion.

Discussion Questions:

1. Think of the last time someone made a You-statement to you. How did you feel?

2. Would you be more likely to change your behavior in response to a You-statement or an I-statement? Why?

3. How do I-statements help people resolve conflicts?

The BIG Mistake
Art and Writing

Objectives:

The students will:

— explore one of many behavior patterns that lead people into conflict.

— understand that people sometimes commit themselves to doing too many things.

— see how conflict can occur when they can't do everything and they let someone down.

— understand how an awareness of this behavior helps people deal constructively with the anger and conflict it causes.

Materials:

drawing and writing material.

Directions:

Read the story, "The Big Mistake," aloud to the children.

Divide the children into two groups.

Ask one group to rewrite the story in a way that shows what would have happened if Elsie had been able to say "no" to one or more of the people who asked her to do things.

Ask the other group to rewrite the story as it might have been if Elsie had been able to admit she had promised to do too many things. Think of something she might have done to help the committee let everyone know about the dance.

Ask volunteers to read their alternative endings.

Conclude by leading a discussion using these and your own questions.

Discussion Questions:

1. Have you ever counted on someone to do something for you and they said, 'yes,' and then let you down?

2. Have you every promised to do something when you knew you really might not be able to get it done? What happened?

3. How did you feel when you didn't do what you had promised to do?

4. How do people generally respond when they feel they have been "let down"?

THE BIG MISTAKE

Elsie was one of the busiest girls in her fifth grade class. She was always doing something-homework or volunteering for work on a committee or helping at home.

Elsie knew it was going to be a particularly busy week for her. Besides her regular homework, she had a big report to write for history and she had volunteered to do a science project for the county fair. She had a piano recital on the weekend and she had to practice every day. Each afternoon right after school she had promised to help her mother bake pies and cakes and cookies for the Church Bazaar.

On Monday, as Elsie was walking down her block to school, Mrs. Page, a neighbor who had just had a new baby, stopped her to ask if she would come over in the evenings to help take care of her three young children. With her new baby taking so much time, Mrs. Page thought it would be nice if Elsie could entertain the older children. Elsie knew she was very busy but she didn't want to say no to Mrs. Page so she agreed to help.

When she got to school, she found out that her class had decided to throw a big dance to raise money for the library. The dance committee asked Elsie if she could write an article and design an ad about the dance for the school paper. Everything had to be ready by Friday morning because that's when the paper was printed. Friday afternoon the papers would be out in time for everyone to see the article for the dance the next night.

It really scared Elsie when she thought about all the things she'd promised to do. But she knew this dance was important and she didn't want to be the only one to say she wouldn't help. So Elsie agreed to do the article and the ad and have them both ready Friday morning.

Friday came sooner than Elsie realized. She really didn't want to go to school that morning because she didn't want to face her classmates. When the committee learned she didn't have the ad and article, they were furious.

Elsie had a lot of excuses ready: She had too much homework to do; she couldn't think of what to say in the article; she didn't like the ad she designed. It wasn't her fault, she told them rather indignantly, that she was so busy. And instead of accepting the blame, she told them she thought they could certainly call all the kids in school to tell them about the dance, or put a notice on the board.

The kids on the committee were really angry with her, as well as very confused about how to tell all the children in school about the dance. They knew one thing: They wouldn't count on Elsie for help again.

A Grumpy Day
Discussion and Writing

Objectives:

The students will:

— understand how negative events can lead to frustration and bad behavior

— become more aware of the dynamics and feelings involved when this happens

— learn to consider alternative ways to handle bad feelings.

Materials:

writing materials

Directions:

Read the story "A Grumpy Day" aloud to the group.

After completing the story, as these and other questions to create discussion.

Discussion Questions:

1. What things happened to Molly before she had a fight with her brother?

2. How do you think Molly was feeling as her brother came into her room?

3. How do you think Molly was feeling after the fight?

4. How do you think Freddie felt after the fight?

5. Have you ever felt the way Molly did and got into a fight with someone?

6. Have you every felt the way Freddie did?

7. How do you think this fight could have been avoided?

Variation:

If time permits, have children write about a time when they had "A Grumpy Day" and got into a conflict. Ask them to tell about what led up to the conflict and how it ended.

A GRUMPY DAY

Molly was lying in her bed, cozy and warm. She was having a dream that made her smile in her sleep. All of a sudden there was a loud knock on her door and someone yelled, "C'mon, Molly. Time to get ready for school."

Molly sat up in bed, rubbing her eyes. Her smile turned into a frown. She got out of bed and accidentally stepped on a book she had been reading the night before. The edge jabbed into her foot. She kicked the book so hard that she hurt her toe.

Taking her favorite, old bathrobe from the chair in the corner, Molly put it on in such a rush that she heard a loud ripping sound. She knew she'd torn the sleeve. As she tried to stretch her neck to look at the rip, she heard another rip coming from the other side. She was so busy looking at her bathrobe that she didn't notice that her dresser drawer was open. She bumped into it and got a big bruise on her leg.

Her bedroom door opened and Molly's little brother Freddie burst in. He asked her in an excited voice, "Could I please borrow a nickle, Molly?" Molly whirled around. She hit him very hard on the shoulder. She yelled, "I told you a hundred times not to come into my room unless you knock first!"

Freddie yelled back, "Gee, I only forgot to knock. That's no reason to hit me. You're really a meanie." He ran out of the room feeling very angry and upset.

Molly was feeling angry too.

What's Bugging You?
Discussion and Art

Objectives:

The students will:
— describe behaviors and situations that bug them and explain how such things can lead to conflict.

— reduce the power that pet peeves have over them by choosing to take positive action.

— explain how taking preventive action can help them avoid conflicts triggered by pet peeves.

Materials:

whiteboard; writing implements; small brown paper bags; newspaper; stapler; colored art paper; scissors; glue; 1- to 2-inch strips of white paper; fine-tip markers

Directions:

Ask the students if they have any pet peeves. Explain that pet peeves are things that annoy or "bug" them. They may be bugged by situations or by people. For example, some students may become annoyed by having to wait in lines, listen to the sound of dripping faucets, or put up with loud TV commercials; others may be bothered when people fail to return borrowed items, gossip about others, or leave belongings scattered around.

Brainstorm with the students the things that "bug" or annoy them. List their pet peeves on the board. The ideas of one student will trigger ideas in the minds of others. After you've developed a fairly long list, explain to the students:

Annoyances like these often lead to conflict or anger outbursts. If you are aware of them and do things to prevent them or to divert your attention from them, you can avoid bad feelings and arguments. For example, maybe your pet peeve is that your brother always leaves his clothes laying on the floor of your shared bedroom. One morning you wake up and realize that you forgot to finish your math homework, so in a panic you jump out of bed and rush to get your backpack. In the process, you stumble over your brother's jeans on the floor. You're not hurt, but you are frustrated and worried about your unfinished homework, so you take your feelings out on your brother by waking him up and shouting at him.

Discuss with the students other examples of conflicts that might arise from pet peeves. Invite the students to describe possible incidents that might be triggered by something that bugs them.

After the brainstorming and discussion, announce that the students will have an opportunity to create their own "bug" out of a brown bag and colored paper. Distribute art materials and suggest that each person create a "perfectly horrible" bug to represent his or her most annoying pet peeve. Give these directions:

First, crumple some newspaper and stuff it into the bag. Next, fold under the open end of the bag and staple, or glue, it closed. Then, use the colored paper to cut out legs, mouth, eyes, antennae, and other markings or features for your bug. Finally, glue these to the stuffed paper bag. When your bug is finished, choose your most annoying pet peeve and write it with a fine-tip marker on a strip of white paper. Glue the white paper strip onto the back of your paper bug.

The next part of the activity may be done over several days: Students pool their brain power to problem solve each other's annoying issues. By working collaboratively, each person ends up with several strategies for

dealing with his or her problem or even eliminating it.

Go around the group and invite the students to share what they wrote and glued on the top of their bugs. After each person shares, ask the rest of the group to suggest strategies to help the person deal with or eliminate the annoyance. For example, someone might say, "The thing that bugs me most is that every time I sit down at the table to do my homework, my little sister wants to play a game or sing to me or scribble on my paper." The group might suggest strategies like:

- Tell her you will play with her for 15 minutes if she promises that afterwards she will go away to let you do your homework.
- Do your homework in your room with the door closed.
- Ask your mom, dad, or another brother or sister to play with her while you finish your homework.
- Give her a pencil and paper and let her do "homework" sitting next to you.
- Do your homework after school in the public library.
- Make a star on a 3"x 5" card for each day she leaves you alone to do your homework and give her a reward for every 5th star.

Suggest that the students refer to the "Conflict Management Strategies" (on page 10) or use any other ideas that might reduce or eliminate the problem. Have the person who shared the problem write suggested solutions on white paper strips, and glue the strips to the underside of his or her bug.

Suggest that each person make an effort to try out one or more of the strategies over the next couple of weeks, write down what happens, and share the results with the group at a later time.

Discussion Questions:

1. How can being aware of what bugs you enable you to avoid anger or resolve conflicts?

2. How can allowing things to continue bugging you (without doing something about them) lead to other, unrelated conflicts or angry feelings?

3. How do you feel when you successfully solve a problem like the one you shared today?

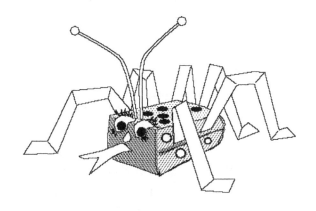

The Behaviors of Conflict
Raising and Lowering the Level of Conflict

Objectives:

The students will:
- identify behaviors that escalate and de-escalate conflict.
- practice using communication skills to control the escalation of conflicts.

Materials:

one copy of the "Arrow" on the last page of this activity for each student

Directions:

In your own words, introduce the concept of conflict escalation and de-escalation. For example, say:

Imagine an escalator, such as the kind you use in department stores. An escalator moves people up and down from one level to another. The same is true with behaviors that escalate and de-escalate conflict. Some words and actions raise, or escalate, anger and conflict to higher levels; other behaviors lower, or de-escalate the anger and conflict, to lower levels. In judging the effects of certain behaviors on conflict, try to picture whether the behavior is making the conflict go up or down.

Distribute a copy of the "Arrow" page to each student. Tell them that you are going to read them two scenarios. As you read, they are to listen closely to the statements and actions of each character in the scenario. When they hear a statement or action that is likely to escalate the conflict, they should hold their arrow high, pointing up. When they hear a statement or action that is likely to de-escalate the conflict, they should hold their arrow pointing down.

Read each scenario slowly, allowing time for the students to respond. Notice if any of the behaviors draw mixed reactions from the students. After you have read each scenario, go back and have the students role play the parts that caused disagreement, with volunteers taking the two roles. Demonstrate and discuss how voice tone, facial expression, and body posture contribute greatly to determining whether a specific behavior is escalating or de-escalating.

Conclude the activity with a general discussion of the concept of anger/conflict escalation and de-escalation.

Extension:

After you have completed the readings and role plays, ask the students to suggest a typical conflict situation that they might face. Write a brief statement describing the situation on the board. Then ask volunteers to role play the characters in the scenario. As director, start the action by feeding the actors some initial dialogue. Then get the class involved, asking volunteers to call out lines that either escalate or de-escalate the conflict. Coach and experiment to demonstrate the effects of various types of actions and statements.

Scenarios:

Scenario #1

Ken and Sue are supposed to be working together to solve a math problem. Ken takes the problem sheet and starts to write his solution on it.

Sue: "Here, let me have that. I think I know how to do this." (Slides the paper away from Ken and starts to write on it.)

Ken: "Hey, I was right in the middle of something. Give that back to me." (Reaches over, pulls the paper back and continues writing.)

Sue: "You're not doing it right, dummy. You're going to have to erase the whole thing."

Ken: "I'll erase your face in a minute if you don't stop bugging me."

Sue: "We're supposed to be doing this together, and you're not listening to me!"

Ken: "Maybe I'd listen if you weren't so pushy. Anyway, I've finished it. There!"

Sue: "It's wrong. You can't prove your answer."

Ken: "Sure I can."

Sue: "Show me, Mr. Smartie. You couldn't prove it if you worked all day. Ha ha ha (loudly)."

Ken: "Shut up, Sue. You always think you know everything, but you don't" (Pushes Sue away.)

Scenario #2

Sergio and Maria are brother and sister. Sergio is watching TV. Maria walks in, picks up the remote control and changes the channel.

Sergio: "Why did you change the channel? I was watching that show!"

Maria: "I don't have time to argue with you. I have to watch this show for my science homework."

Sergio: "I don't care what it's for. That was my favorite show. Change it back right now!"

Maria: "You can't make me. I have just as much right to this TV as you do."

Sergio: "Not if I'm here first. I'm telling Mom!"

Maria: "Go ahead and tell Mom, cry baby. She'll just make you go do your homework."

Sergio: "I finished mine. What's the science program about?"

Maria: "Insects. Like you, creepy brother."

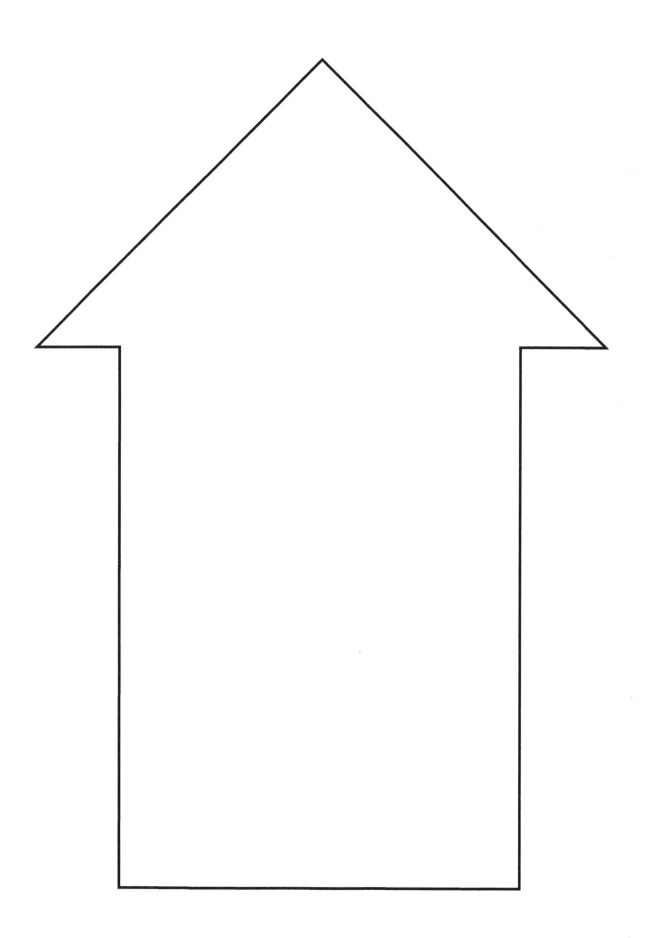

The Language of Conflict
Writing, Discussion, and Role Play

Objectives:

The students will:

— write a conflict dialogue, mapping the escalation of the conflict from verbal sparring to physical violence.

— alter the dialogue to show how different words can change the direction of the conflict.

— practice using calming vocabulary in stressful situations.

Materials:

chart paper and markers; writing materials for the students

Directions:

Have the students form pairs and decide on a conflict that they would like to script. This could be based on a real life conflict that they experienced or saw (Remind them not to use real names.), or it could be a conflict they viewed on TV, in a movie, or game. It can also be a made-up conflict. Explain that you want them to write a dialogue typical of the conflict they have selected.

Circulate and coach the students, helping them identify the words of the conflict, and through written dialogue, map the escalation of the conflict from verbal to physical fighting. If time allows, have each pair script two conflict episodes in this manner.

When the students have finished writing, ask them to help you develop a list of vocabulary associated with conflict. They should be able to take the words directly from their written dialogues. Record the words on chart paper so that the list can be saved. Expect statements like:

No!
Shut up!
It's mine!
I had it first!
You nerd!
Stupid!

Note: When students want to express cussing or foul language in their scripts, they do so with stars (***) and exclamation marks (!!!).

Next, turn the attention of the students to the language of peaceful conflict resolution. Have each pair take its first conflict dialogue and, at the point where the conflict is well established, begin to change the words, showing what must happen in order to end the conflict peacefully. When the pairs have finished with the first dialogue, have them rewrite the second one as well.

Chart the peaceful vocabulary in the same manner as the conflict vocabulary.

Use the remaining time to role play some of the peaceful conflict resolution dialogues.

Note: Once the students understand the contrast between conflict vocabulary and resolution vocabulary and have scripted conflict dialogues, keep the focus on peaceful conflict resolution.

Discussion Questions:

1. Was it easy or hard to change your dialogue to include peaceful vocabulary? Why?

2. How hard do you think it is to change the type of words you're using in a real conflict situation? What do you think would make it easier?

3. How will this exercise help you resolve your own conflicts?

Variation:

At lower grade levels, develop the dialogue as a total group, with the students contributing ideas, and you recording.

The Cause and Effect of Conflict
Brainstorm and Group Discussion

Objectives:

The students will:

— describe possible effects of prescribed events.

— explain that they can choose behaviors that produce positive outcomes to events, thereby avoiding conflict

Materials:

one copy of each event (provided) written on a strip of paper; writing paper and pencils

Directions:

Talk with the students about how certain events can cause subsequent things to happen, creating a chain of events that can sometimes have very negative consequences. In your own words, explain:

Very often, one event in life actually causes another event to happen. For example, in a conflict situation the behavior of one person often causes another person to react. The second person's reaction then causes the first person to react. These back-and-forth reactions continue until an argument or fight develops. For example, you might be walking through the mall with a friend and she tells you something funny. You start to laugh just as you approach another friend. That friend thinks you are laughing at her, so she snubs you. Then you get mad and call her a snob — and so on until the situation becomes a conflict. Ask the students if they have ever experienced anything like this.

Tell the students that in this activity they will brainstorm logical causes of an event. They will then brainstorm logical effects of the same event. Explain that this will help them become more aware of how some conflicts happen and how those conflicts can be prevented.

Divide the students into small groups. Give each group one strip of paper with an event written on it. Ask the groups to brainstorm possible causes of their event. Tell them to write all ideas down on paper so that they can be shared with the entire class. Give the students a few minutes to complete this task; then ask the groups to turn their paper over and write possible effects of the same event on the other side. Ask the students to brainstorm as many possible causes and effects as they can.

Ask each group to share both "cause" and "effects" with the class. Help the students distinguish between the positive and negative causes and effects, and invite them to predict which effects would probably lead to anger and conflict. In your own words, point out:

All of the events have the potential for becoming conflicts. However, if you are involved in an event like one of these, you can prevent conflict by choosing to react positively instead of negatively.

If any group has not listed at least one positive effect for its event, ask the other students to help think of one. Emphasize that each person has a choice to change the course of many events in life so that they are positive.

Discussion Questions:

1. Why is it important for us to be aware of causes and effects?

2. How can we change the course of an event so that a conflict is averted or anger doesn't erupt and get out of control?

3. What can you do to stop yourself from reacting negatively to a situation which upsets you?

Events

1. Your brother storms out of the house and slams the front door.

————————————————————————————

2. You get to the ball park only to remember that you left your catcher's mitt on the kitchen table.

————————————————————————————

3. The person sitting next to you at school announces that his lunch money is missing from his desk.

————————————————————————————

4. You can't go to the movies with your friend on Saturday.

————————————————————————————

5. You had a bad day at school.

————————————————————————————

6. Dad asks you to mow the lawn two Saturdays in row.

————————————————————————————

7. Your teacher says you didn't turn in your homework and you could have sworn that you did.

————————————————————————————

8. Your best friend eats lunch with someone else.

————————————————————————————

9. The coach calls you off the field and asks you to sit out the rest of the game.

————————————————————————————

10. A friend borrows your math book and doesn't return it the day before a test

The Other Side of the Story
The Role of Perspective and Motive in Conflict

Objectives:

The students will:

— state that two people can see the same incident very differently and explain how that happens.

— demonstrate how easy it is to mistake the motives and misinterpret the actions of others.

— explain how misunderstandings about motive lead to conflict.

Materials:

copies of the story, "The Maligned Wolf," to assist older students during the role play (optional)

Directions:

With minimal introduction, read the story "The Maligned Wolf" to the students. After the first few lines, most students will catch on to the fact that they are hearing "Little Red Riding Hood" told from a completely different perspective — the wolf's.

When you have finished the story, ask the students for their reactions. Point out that the story represents one author's explanation for why the wolf behaved the way he did, and that other authors attempting the same thing would probably imagine different scenarios.

Role play the story. Invite volunteers to take the parts of the wolf, little girl, grandmother, and lumberjack. Also implied at the end of the story are countless citizens who develop a fear of wolves because of the incident described, begin to hunt wolves, and ultimately cause the wolf to become an endangered specie. "Extras" can represent these elements of the story in creative ways.

After the students have experienced the plausibility of there being an explanation for the wolf's behavior, turn the discussion to the subject of conflict. Ask the students how many times they have become angry, hurt, or resentful because of something a person said or did, without stopping to wonder what that person's reasons might be. Focus on the fact that both people in a conflict have reasons or motives for their actions.

Note: The next activity, "Understanding the Other Point of View," further explores the concept of individual perspective as it relates to conflict. Implementing the two activities in sequence greatly reinforces student learning.

Discussion Questions:

1. The two sides of this story were very different. Do you think this ever happens in real life? How?

2. You may have heard the popular saying, "There are two sides to every story." What does it mean?

3. Why is it important to try to understand the other person's side of a situation?

4. If you are having a conflict with someone, what are some ways of finding out how that person sees things?

5. Why do we frequently act as though our side of a conflict is the only side?

The Maligned Wolf

By Leif Fearn

The forest was my home. I lived there and I cared about it. I tried to keep it neat and clean.

Then one sunny day, while I was cleaning up some garbage a camper had left behind, I heard footsteps. I leaped behind a tree and saw a rather plain little girl coming down the trail carrying a basket. I was suspicious of this little girl right away because she was dressed funny — all in red, and her head covered up so it seemed like she didn't want people to know who she was. Naturally, I stopped to check her out. I asked who she was, where she was going, where she had come from, and all that.

She gave me a song and dance about going to her grandmother's house with a basket of lunch. She appeared to be a basically honest person, but she was in my forest and she certainly looked suspicious with that strange getup of hers. So I decided to teach her just how serious it is to prance through the forest unannounced and dressed funny.

I let her go on her way, but I ran ahead to her grandmother's house. When I saw that nice old woman, I explained my problem and she agreed that her granddaughter needed to learn a lesson, all right. The old woman agreed to stay out of sight until I called her. Actually, she hid under the bed.

When the girl arrived, I invited her into the bedroom where I was in the bed, dressed like the grandmother. The girl came in all rosy-cheeked and said something nasty about my big ears. I've been insulted before so I made the best of it by suggesting that my big ears would help me to hear better. Now, what I meant was that I liked her and wanted to pay close attention to what she was saying. But she makes another insulting crack about my bulging eyes. Now you can see how I was beginning to feel about this girl who put on such a nice front, but was apparently a very nasty person. Still, I've made it a policy to try to ignore put-downs, so I told her that my big eyes helped me to see her better.

Her next insult really got to me. I've got this problem with having big teeth. And that little girl made an insulting crack about them. I know that I should have had better control, but I leaped up from that bed and growled that my teeth would help me to eat her better.

Now let's face it — no wolf has ever eaten a little girl — everyone knows that. But that crazy girl started running around the house screaming, with me chasing her trying to calm her down. I'd taken off the grandmother clothes, but that only seemed to make things worse.

All of a sudden the door came crashing open and a big lumberjack was standing there with his ax. I looked at him and all of a sudden it became clear that I was in deep trouble. There was an open window behind me and out I went.

I'd like to say that was the end of it. But that grandmother character never did tell my side of the story. Before long the word got around that I was a terrible, mean guy. Everybody started shooting at me. I don't know about that little girl with the funny red outfit, but I didn't live happily ever after. In fact, now we wolves are an endangered specie. And I'm sure that little girl's story has had a lot to do with it!

Understanding the Other Point of View
Partner Talk and Discussion

Objectives:

The students will:

— describe two different perceptions of a conflict situation.

— state that every conflict situation has more than one point of view.

— describe how understanding all points of view can help resolve conflicts.

Materials:

two pieces of drawing paper per student; colored markers, pencils or crayons; a version of the story of the "Three Little Pigs"; for the optional extension: one copy of the 1995, Newberry Award winning book, "Walk Two Moons," by Sharon Creech (1994, Harper Collins)

Directions:

Ask the students if they are familiar with the story of The Three Little

Pigs. Invite them to review the plot with you. Younger children may enjoy listening to you read the story aloud. (Many versions are available both in books and online.) Explain that most stories can have more than one point of view. The Maligned Wolf, from the previous activity, is told from the wolf's point of view. If you have not previously read this story, read it to the students now, and discuss how completely different the story seems from the wolf's perspective. In your own words, elaborate:

When you are in a conflict, the other person's point of view, or perception, is often overshadowed by your own. Making an effort to understand the other point of view may help to resolve the conflict. An old Indian saying states that you can't judge another person until you have walked two moons (months) in his moccasins. In this activity, you will put yourself in the moccasins of another person and try to imagine his or her side of a conflict.

Before having the students choose partners, give each person two pieces of drawing paper and some colored pencils, markers, or crayons. Provide these directions:

Draw the <u>top</u> view of a large pair of moccasins. Make the outline of the left moccasin on one sheet of paper and the right moccasin on the other sheet. Next, put a symbol or design in colors on the top forward part of each shoe. Use colored dots to represent beads and make your design stand for something about you. Finally, cut out both moccasins. Make the moccasins extra large so that they may be seen easily when placed on the floor.

When the moccasins are finished, ask the students to think of a conflict that they have had with another person, — one in which they had a very clear point of view. Caution the students to choose a conflict that they are willing to share with a partner. Give the students time to think carefully about the conflict, writing it down on paper if necessary.

After each person has chosen a conflict, explain that in this activity the students will have a chance to look at that conflict from the other person's viewpoint, like "walking in another person's moccasins."

Have the students form dyads. Give these instructions:

Place your paper moccasins on the floor toe-to-toe with your partner's moccasins. Stand on your set of moccasins, facing your partner, and decide who is A and who is B. A's, you will tell your conflict story to your partner. Express your point of view very clearly to your partner, including any personal feelings you have about the conflict. B's, your job is to suggest ways in which the story can be told from the other person's viewpoint. What would the other person in this conflict want? How would he or she feel?

Give the students time to carry out your directions. Then continue:

Now I want you to switch places with your partner. Stand on your partners moccasins. A's, retell your conflict experience, this time from the perspective of the other person. Recall the ideas your partner gave you and try to express the other person's thoughts, opinions, and feelings. B's, listen carefully. When your partner is finished telling the story from the other person's perspective, tell your partner how you think he or she did. Was your partner convincing? Did your partner really seem to be walking in the other person's moccasins?

Have the partners return to their own moccasins and repeat the activity with the B's acting as storytellers. When both partners have had a turn as conflict storyteller, ask several volunteers to share their stories with the whole group. Coach each volunteer to tell his or her story from both perspectives. Debrief the activity with a discussion concerning the importance of seeing the other person's point of view — particularly in a conflict.

Note: To ensure the success of this activity, you may need to demonstrate the dyad procedure with a volunteer.

Extension:

As a follow up to this activity, older students may enjoy reading (or hearing you read) Sharon Creech's Walk Two Moons. In this story, Salamanca, a thirteen-year-old girl, experiences many internal conflicts. When Salamanca's mother leaves her and her father; she promises to return but doesn't. At the end of the story, Sal and her grandfather play a game in which they take turns pretending to walk in someone else's moccasins. They talk about how they would feel and what they would do.

Discussion Questions:

1. Was it easy or hard to "walk in the other person's moccasins" and tell the story from his or her point of view? Why?

2. Why is it important to think about a conflict from different points of view?

3. How can thinking about the other person's point of view help you avoid or resolve a conflict?

Taking the Other Point of View
Role-playing Different Positions in Conflict Situations

Objective:

The students will:

— role-play and observe opposing positions in a conflict situation,

— gain insight into the validity of opposing points of view.

Materials:

a copy of one skit from Conflict Skits for each team

Directions:

Divide the students into teams of two and assign each team one of the conflict skits.

Explain to the students that each team will have an opportunity to role-play the skit they've been given..

Have each team read its situation and then select the point of view each partner will act out.

Ask each team to act out its situation for the entire class.

After each skit has continued long enough for each child to get into his or her part, say Stop and ask the actors to exchange roles. Remind them what their point of view will now be. Then allow them to continue to role-play the scene long enough for each to identify with the new point of view. Stop the drama again before an ending is reached.

After each skit, ask each participant:

a. When you were acting your first part, how did you feel about the other person?

b. In your first role did you believe you were right?

c. After you switched roles, how did you feel?

d. What did you think of the point of view of the second character after you played that part?

e. After you played both sides, did you think that only one side was right or wrong?

After each skit, ask the following
questions or those of your own to the
entire group.

a. What did you see happening in
   this skit?

b. What happened to the actors
   when they had to play the part
   of the other person?

c. After seeing both actors play
   both roles do you think that only
   one side was right or wrong?

CONFLICT SKITS

PLOT ONE - Two characters:

Situation: Child A borrows a sweater from Child B, promising to take good care of it; but when Child B gets the sweater back, it has a hole in it.

Viewpoint of Child A:

The sweater got torn when someone else grabbed at it. It was an accident. I meant to take good care of it.

Viewpoint of Child B:

It was a good sweater, and I trusted you to take care of it. You were careless.

— —

PLOT TWO - Two characters:

Situation: Child A wants to borrow a CD from Child B for a party. The CD is a rare one and a favorite of everyone's, especially Child B's. Child B says no.

Viewpoint of Child A:

I need the CD so my party will be a hit. I'll take good care of it by putting it in a safe place when it's not being played.

Viewpoint of Child B:

The CD can never be replaced. There will be a lot of people at the party, and I'm afraid it will get lost or damaged.

PLOT THREE - Two characters:

Situation: Child A asks a sister (B) to tell Mom (C) that he is going to stay after school to make up a test and will get home late. Sister B forgets and Mom is angry at them both.

Viewpoint of Child A:

It was important for me to stay and make up the test. I trusted my sister to tell Mom. I'm really mad at her for forgetting to do it.

Viewpoint of Mom C.-

It really makes me angry that no one remembered to tell me that he would be late getting home from school. I got very concerned and I spent a lot of time worrying instead of doing other things that needed to be done.

— —

PLOT FOUR -   Two characters:

Situation: Child A, a girl, is playing baseball and hits the ball very hard. When she throws the bat down, it hits child B, a boy, in the leg.

Viewpoint of Child A:

It was an accident. I thought I'd hit a home run. He was standing where nobody's supposed to stand. If he had been in the right place he wouldn't have gotten hit.

Viewpoint of Child B:

My leg got hurt. The rules say that you shouldn't throw the bat because people get hurt that way.

Learning Conflict Resolution Strategies
Presentation and Comprehension Check

Objectives:

The students will:

— explain strategies for handling conflicts in their own words.

— identify the conflict strategies used in stories.

— create stories as examples of strategies

Materials:

one set of copies (one per student) of each of the nine conflict management strategies provided at the end of this activity.

Directions:

Introduce the activity by inviting the students to think about a time when they were involved in a conflict or observed a conflict. Suggest that they think about the events leading up to the conflict and the feelings of the people involved in the conflict.

Have the students choose partners and tell each other their conflict stories. After the pairs have shared,

invite a few volunteers to retell their experiences to the entire group.

Explain that certain behaviors can help people to handle disagreements more positively and to resolve their conflicts. These behaviors are called strategies.

Have the students get back together with their partners. If you have made copies of the conflict management strategy pages from the book, distribute them to the students. A list of the strategies also appears on page 10. This can provide you with an explanation of each strategy to share with the students. Present and explain the first conflict resolution strategy (Listen to the Other Person) and give an example of a situation in which it might be used. Examine each of the remaining strategies in the same manner:

• Explain your position without blaming the other person.

• Allow time to cool off.

- Problem solve together to create a "win-win" situation.

- Be willing to compromise.

- Say you're sorry.

- Use humor.

- Ask for help.

- Know when to walk away.

After all of the strategies have been presented and explained, check for comprehension. Read the following nine scenarios and, after each one, ask the students to identify the strategy used. If the students have copies of the conflict management strategy pages, ask them to hold up the page that shows the strategy used in that scenario, and point to the specific strategy.

When the students have shown that they understand and can identify all nine strategies, invite them to create new scenarios to represent each one. Either assign one strategy to each existing pair of students or ask the students to form small groups and create stories for two or more of the strategies. Have the students read or perform their scenario(s) and ask the other students to identify the strategies used. Conclude the activity by facilitating further discussion about the strategies.

Discussion Questions:

1. Which of the strategies do you find easiest to use and why? Which are hardest for you?

2. Why is it better to choose a strategy to deal with a conflict, rather than just react automatically?

3. What will help you remember these strategies when you are angry or in the middle of a conflict?

Conflict Resolution Scenarios

Scenario #1

Cherisse waited half an hour after school for her friend Jonelle, who had promised to walk home with her. Cherisse and Jonelle had made the arrangement at lunch time. After waiting 30 minutes, Cherisse went to Jonelle's classroom and asked the teacher if Jonelle had left yet. The teacher said that Jonelle had run out of the room as soon as class was dismissed. When Cherisse saw Jonelle walking towards her the next morning, she was so angry and hurt that she ignored her. Jonelle ran after her, saying, "Let me explain, please!" Finally Cherisse thought that maybe she should listen to what Cherisse had to say. Maybe she had a good reason for leaving school suddenly. Sure enough, Jonelle explained that, just before the end of school, she remembered that her mom had told her to get home fast for an appointment with the dentist. She further explained that her mom threatened to ground her if she came home late. Cherisse was glad that she listened to Jonelle carefully instead of losing a friendship over hurt feelings. (Listen carefully to the other person.)

Scenario #2

Marco and his cousin Lidia lived close to each other and they shared a bike. They agreed to use the bike alternately, Marco one week, Lidia the next. One week Lidia forgot to return the bike to Marco and she went riding off to a friend's house. Marco was counting on using the bike to ride to soccer practice and couldn't find Lidia or the bike. He was very upset. When Lidia returned home on the bike, Marco started screaming at her and grabbed the bike away from her. Lidia remembered two occasions when Marco forgot to return the bike to her so she started yelling back. They were both losing their tempers. Finally Lidia said, "Take the bike. We can talk this over after we've had time to cool off. How about tomorrow after school?" (Allow time to cool off.)

Scenario #3

Arjel thought that his classmate Kenny was to blame for the class losing 10 minutes of free time. Kenny was talking to someone in his group about the homework after the teacher told the class to be quiet. Others were talking and giggling, too, but Arjel only saw Kenny talking. After school, Arjel stomped out of class grumbling to himself. When Kenny asked why he was so mad, Arjel wanted to put the blame on him for the loss of free time, but he replied instead, "I'm really mad that we missed our free time. I was working on a picture for the art fair and wanted to finish it today. I'm upset that everyone couldn't get quiet when the teacher asked us to." (Explain your position without blaming the other person.)

Scenario #4

When Jessica struck out at bat in the bottom of the ninth inning , she felt terrible. Her friend and classmate, Nina, made it worse by blaming her for the team's loss. "We could have won, Jess," shrilled Nina. "Why didn't you try a little harder to hit the ball? Geez, now we're out of the playoffs!" Jessica wanted to cry, but she knew that the team's loss wasn't her fault alone. She took a deep breath and said, "I'm really sorry that we lost the game, Nina. I feel bad, and I know you do, too. That pitcher was sure awesome." (Say you're sorry.)

Scenario #5

When Kyle accidentally tripped over Andy's foot walking into the assembly, he didn't have a chance to apologize because his teacher was hurrying the class to their seats. He felt nervous because he knew Andy was short-tempered. On the way back to class, Andy went up to Kyle, pushed him and accused Kyle of kicking him deliberately. When Kyle tried to explain, Andy pushed him again. Kyle said firmly, "Hey, I'm not interested in fighting," and headed for the classroom before Andy could hurt him. (Know when to walk away.)

Scenario #6

The two groups of boys faced each other on the basketball court. It was lunch recess and both groups wanted to use the full court for a game.

"We have a problem here," said Darcy, "Can't we work something out?"

"O.K., you play half court with your teams and we'll play the other half," replied Mai Lei.

Jimmy chimed in, "That's not as fun as playing full court. Why don't you guys use the whole court for ten minutes; then we can play on it for the remaining ten."

"I have another idea," said Darcy. "We can play each other using the full court and rotate players in and out every time a basket is made. That way we all get a chance to play full court."

"Sounds like an idea," answered Jimmy. "What do you think, guys?" (Problem solve together to create a "win-win" situation.)

Scenario #7

Mr. Cruz was returning homework and test papers. Mindy glanced at the paper that was passed back to her. Thinking that it was her homework, she began tearing it up. When Ahmed looked over her shoulder and saw that it was his math test, he shouted, "Hey, what are you doing with my test? My dad wants to see all of my test grades!" Surprised and embarrassed, Mindy stared at the shredded paper and put her hands to her reddened face.

"Oh...," she giggled, "I knew that. I thought your dad liked putting together jigsaw puzzles." (Using humor if the situation calls for it.)

Scenario #8

Brad and his sister Farah were playing ping pong at the recreation center on Saturday afternoon. They were using the paddles that they checked out from the equipment room. Two girls came into the room and started looking around for something. "Wait a minute, here they are," exclaimed one of the girls. "Those two are using them."

"Hey, give us back the ping-pong paddles," the other one said to Farah and Brad, "I left them on this table two days ago."

Brad answered defensively, "They can't be yours. We checked them out of the equipment room just a few minutes ago."

"I don't care where you got them," replied the girl, "They're mine and I want them back."

"Hold on," said Farah, we'd better go to the recreation leader and ask her to help with this problem.

"Fine by me," answered the girl.

(Ask for help when you need it.)

Scenario #9

Ben and his brother Adam promised not to argue or fight if Mom took them for a day hike in the mountains. Both were excited about spotting birds and recording them so they could earn their nature badges in scouts. Mom had only one pair of binoculars and warned the boys that they would have to share them on the hike. Adam talked to Ben before the hike, "Look, man, I really need to record more birds than you. Let me hold the binoculars, and after I see a bird on my list, I'll pass the glasses on to you."

"Wait a minute," answered Ben calmly.

"It wasn't my fault that you lost your last check list. I think that we should compromise. You carry the glasses for half an hour; then I'll get them for half an hour. The person holding the glasses will get to see a bird first before passing them to the other person. That way, whoever holds the binoculars knows he'll see the bird before it flies away."

"All right," shrugged Adam. "I guess that's only fair. Then we won't argue and get Mom upset." (Be willing to compromise.)

Conflict Management Strategies

Conflict Management Strategies

Cooling Off
Discussion and Pantomime

Objectives:

The students will:

— describe positive ways of cooling off to prevent a conflict.

— explain how a cooling-off period can help prevent conflict.

Materials:

chart paper and marking pens; for each group

Directions:

Refer to the conflict management strategies (pages 90-92), drawing attention to the strategy which suggests a cooling-off period be allowed if the people involved in a conflict are extremely angry, tired, or out of control. Explain to the students that sometimes all that is required is a little time for tempers to cool; then the parties involved can handle the conflict in a positive way. Other times, people may need to take some kind of positive action in order to calm down, such as taking a bike ride around the park or listening to calming music. Another possibility is to take a nap; still another is to literally cool off in the shower, under a hose, or in a swimming pool.

Divide the students into small groups (3 to 5) and ask them to think of things they sometimes do to cool off when they are upset or angry. Give each group a sheet of chart paper and a marking pen and explain:

You will have about 5 minutes to list as many cooling-off activities as you can think of. Write down the activities you use, activities you have seen other people use, and new *activities that you haven't tried but think might work for you. Write down only realistic ideas that you could use in everyday life.*

Call time after about 5 minutes. Quickly poll the groups to see how many cooling-off activities they have recorded. If additional time is needed, allow the students a few more minutes to complete the task. Then invite each group to hold up its list and share it with the rest of the students. While each group is reading its list, instruct the other groups to check items on their own lists that match those being read aloud. After the groups have shared, talk about the most popular cooling-off activities. Ask the students to explain why those activities might also be the most effective ones.

Play a pantomime game to give the students an opportunity to rehearse some of the cooling-off activities. Ask a volunteer to stand in front of the group and silently act out, or pantomime, one of the ways to cool off and avoid conflict. Allow time for the volunteer to complete the action. Then ask the rest of the group to guess the cooling-off activity. Have the performing student choose another volunteer to pantomime a different activity. Continue this process until all of the most popular activities have been acted out.

Smaller children may enjoy a "follow-the leader" variation of this game. Have the children stand in a large circle facing each other and ask a volunteer to pantomime a cooling-off activity. After the action is completed and the group has guessed what the activity is, have the volunteer repeat the action while the rest of the group mirrors it. Then have the volunteer choose another child to be the leader.

Discussion Questions:

1. Why are some cooling-off activities more effective than others?

2. How can bringing these activities to our attention now help prevent a conflict later?

3. In what kinds of situations might a cooling-off time be most effective?

All About Endings
Experience Sheet and Role Play

Objectives:

The students will:

— recognize and interpret common conflict situations.

— role play a conflict from beginning to end, and be able to explain its direction and ending.

Materials:

one copy of the Experience Sheet, "How Will This Conflict End?" for each student

Directions:

In this activity, students develop conflict situations using only the visual cues found in four cartoons. Teams are formed, and each team develops a skit around one of the conflict situations. The skits are performed for the total group, and a discussion concludes the activity.

Distribute the Experience Sheets and go over the directions. Give the students a few minutes to fill in the dialogue bubbles. When they have finished, ask the students to form groups of three or four. In your own words, explain the assignment:

First, take a few minutes to share what you have written in the dialogue bubbles with the members of your team. Second, decide which of the four situations you want to act out. Third, agree on what the conflict is about, and together, write a script demonstrating what the disputants do and how the conflict ends. When you have finished your script, assign roles and take a few minutes to rehearse. One team member should be the director.

Allow time for sharing, planning, writing and rehearsing. Then have the teams perform their skits for the group. Facilitate a brief discussion after each performance, using the questions below and others that are generated by the skit.

Discussion Questions:

To the performing team:

1. Did all members of the team interpret the cartoon the same way? If not, how did you resolve your different perceptions?

2. What did you want to show us about conflict through your skit?

To the total group:

1. What was this conflict about?

2. What were the needs of the people involved?

3. What happened in the conflict and how did it end?

4. Have you ever been involved in a conflict like this? How did your conflict end?

How Will This Conflict End?
Experience Sheet

Look at the four pictures that follow. Fill in the dialogue bubbles with the words you think the people are saying or thinking.

Your Challenge:

With your teammates, select one of the cartoons. Write a skit telling what happens in the conflict, and how the conflict ends.

Tell a Story in Pictures
Cartoon Drawing

Objectives:

The students will:

— draw a cartoon depicting a situation that could lead to a conflict.

— demonstrate their knowledge of strategies for handling conflicts by using one or more strategies to resolve their cartoon story.

Materials:

examples of cartoons depicting conflict; white drawing paper cut in half or thirds lengthwise; rulers; pencils; colored pencils, markers, or crayons

Directions:

Introduce this activity by telling the students that it is possible to tell stories about conflict situations by drawing cartoons. Distribute several examples of cartoons from the newspaper and have the students examine the variety of artistic styles and the ways in which cartoonists convey their stories, messages, and ideas.

Explain to the students that to make their own cartoon, they first need to think of a simple story. In your own words, say to them:

Think about a conflict situation which you have experienced, observed, or imagined. Focus on the events that led up to the situation, what each person did, and how the conflict ended. If the conflict had a positive ending, show it the way it happened. If it did not have a positive ending, change the story so that the conflict is resolved in a positive way. For example, show the characters using one of the conflict-resolution strategies that you have learned about.

Make up characters to represent the real people in your story. Your characters can be animals, small children, or thematic characters such as a queen with her court, pirates, Vikings, or witches. Give your characters exaggerated features, such as a large nose, messy hair, or short arms and legs. Your characters can deliver the same message as in a realistic story; however, because they are fictional, they will lend a light-hearted humor to the real-life situation you are illustrating.

The setting of a cartoon is very important. Create a setting that reflects the mood of the story. Focus on important details; don't confuse the reader with too many extras. For example, if you want to show the passage of time from morning to night, show the same scene with the same objects at different times of day. If all of the action in your story occurs in the same place over a short period of time, show the setting from a distance in the first frame and closer in each consecutive frame. The same applies to characters. Draw the first frame showing full bodies; then zoom in closer and closer with each consecutive frame, ending the cartoon with faces, mouths or eyes only . Or reverse the process, starting close and panning out.

Distribute the strips of paper and drawing materials. Before drawing, coach the students to mentally divide their story into four or five parts. Give them an opportunity to sketch out their story on scratch paper, using four to five frames (made by dividing a strip of paper into squares). If four frames are used, have the students fold their strip in half, then in half again. Five frames require the students to measure and divide. Coach the students to keep their story simple and to the point by thinking carefully about what they want their characters to say and do in each frame.

Post the completed cartoons on the board, or make a book by stapling or binding all of the cartoons together between brightly decorated covers.

Note: As an alternate art activity, have the students make posters representing one or more of the strategies for managing conflict outlined in this book. Or have them illustrate positive strategies of their own creation.

Discussion Questions:

1. Was it easier or more difficult to tell your story using cartoon characters? Why?

2. Why does telling a story in cartoon form make people pay closer attention to the story or message?

3. What did you learn about positive conflict resolution strategies from this activity?

Journal Writing
Tips for Adult Leaders

Why Keep Journals?

Journal keeping is a vehicle for building self-awareness, personal insight, and self-esteem, and is an excellent means of developing skills for managing anger and handling conflict creatively and effectively. Verbal skills, reading comprehension, and written expression are developed through regular writing, while journal writing stimulates visual thinking and perceiving.

Throughout the course of this book, students participate in activities that involve conflict resolution and anger management strategies. These activities are largely social (interpersonal), involving large group, small group and partner interactions. These interactions are important because they allow students to practice pro-social strategies cooperatively and creatively, and to realize through their own experience that all persons can emerge from conflict as winners. However, students also have an "inner voice" (intrapersonal) that often reflects on external events, interactions, and behaviors. This intrapersonal component includes private thoughts, feelings and dreams. It may be a side of each child not readily shared with others; however it too can be developed and brought to a level of individual awareness.

Journal writing encourages students to express their innermost feelings in a private, non judgmental atmosphere. It allows the release of pent-up emotions that may have no other outlet. In times of anger or conflict, a child can discharge in writing much of the turbulence within and even creatively explore solutions to problems. Drawing on their own thoughts, feelings and experiences, students can explore added dimensions to anger management and conflict resolution. These personal experiences, beliefs, and insights can make learning interactive strategies more relevant and durable.

Make or Designate Journals

Journals can be made from pieces of lined or unlined paper stapled or bound together. They can be composition books, spiral or loose-leaf notebooks, or bound blank books. The journal can also be written on the computer and kept there or hard copies can be printed and bound into book form. Students write and/or draw pictures to represent their ideas.

Use Journals Regularly

Journal writing draws on the thoughts, feelings and experiences of the students to help them gain better insights into anger and conflicts and how to resolve them. Therefore, you might want to assign journal writing as a follow-up for each group activity. Journal writing can also be done weekly for a set amount of time, or as homework.

You can ask the students to respond to a given topic or question, record their own conflict resolution experiences, or just write "stream-of-consciousness" thoughts.

Responding to topics or questions: The questions below can be used to stimulate writing as follow-up to most of the interactive activities in this book:

— What did you learn from this activity?
— How did this activity make it easier for you to prevent or handle conflicts (or anger)?
— How can you use, right now, the strategies learned in this activity?

— Have you ever used the strategies learned in this activity? How?
— How do you feel about what happened in this activity? Why?

Keeping a conflict or anger record: Have the students write about personal experiences involving conflict and anger. Decide whether you want them to record all experiences or only those in which they successfully use positive strategies. Later, you can ask the students to voluntarily share some of these experiences in small groups. As an alternative, have the students record their use of the strategies in chart form. Show them how to use a two-page spread in the journal to set up a chart. Have them measure ten equal horizontal columns, nine for the prescribed strategies and one additional column for "other" strategies. Then have them draw narrow vertical columns across the chart, creating a grid where they can record the dates on which they use the various strategies. Elaborations of each conflict experience may be written on subsequent pages and dated to correspond to the chart.

Recording a stream of consciousness: If students have no difficulty putting their thoughts on paper, you may simply assign the task of writing for a set amount of time about anything related to the conflict or anger theme. Often this open-ended approach produces surprising insights and creative ideas for solving problems.

Establish a Quiet Atmosphere

It is important to choose a quiet, relaxing environment for the journal-writing process. As much as possible, eliminate distractions, noise, and interruptions. If students are keeping journals for homework, suggest that they choose a quiet atmosphere free from distracting noises like TV, people talking, or loud music.

Make It a Safe Activity

By making journal writing a safe venue for creative expression — immune to failure, ridicule, and grading — you are better able to promote writing as a fulfilling and enjoyable activity. A journal is a place to nurture creativity and emotional development, not rigid standards of spelling and grammar.

Honor Confidentiality

Ideally, journals are confidential. If you are going to read the journals, let the students know ahead of time. Suggest that students fold over any page that they do not want you to read. Or ask them to write strictly private thoughts in a separate location.

Sharing Circle and Role-Play Process
Guidelines for Leaders

The Sharing Circle and role-play process allows students to share a variety of ideas and experiences related to conflict and anger, choose one of those experiences to role-play, brainstorm alternate endings, and role-play at least one positive alternative. By adhering to the following procedures when leading this process, you can ensure that it runs smoothly and effectively.

Part I:
Sharing Circle

1. **Establish ground rules for discussion:** The specific Sharing Circle rules must be followed for this type of discussion. Explain their importance to the students prior to introducing the topic.

   ### The Sharing Circle Rules

   - Every person gets one turn to talk, including the leader.
   - You can skip your turn if you wish.
   - Listen to the person who is sharing.
   - There are no interruptions, probing, put-downs, or gossip.
   - The time is shared equally.

2. **Introduce the Sharing Circle topic:** Elaborate on the topic so the students can focus on what you would like them to talk about. (Specific Sharing Circle topics and suggested elaborations are provided, beginning on page 107.) Give the students time to think before they begin sharing.

3. **Conduct the Sharing Circle where everyone gets a chance to talk to the topic:** Ask the students to share their experiences and related feelings. (You share, too.) Be sure to follow the established Sharing Circle rules listed above.

Part II:
Role Play

1. **Choose one incident to role-play.** After everyone has had an opportunity to share in the Sharing Circle, ask the group to select one of the shared experiences to dramatize. The selected incident should:

   • have one clear-cut moment of conflict.

   • involve two or more people.

   • be resolvable through the use of positive conflict resolution strategies.

2. **Have the story-teller repeat the incident.** The student whose incident is chosen retells the story so that everyone has a clear picture of what occurred and the roles of the people involved.

3. **Role-play the incident up to the point of conflict.** Select volunteers to act out the scenario leading up to the point at which the conflict occurs. The student whose story is chosen should arrange the actors on a "stage," describe the setting, and add helpful props (optional). If the story is based on personal experience, the storyteller may play him/herself. Coach the actors, encouraging them to become as realistically involved as possible. Employ the following prompts, as needed:

   —What expression would you have on your face in this situation?

   — What words would you say and how would you say them?

   —How did the other person(s) react to what you said or did?

   —Think about how your character felt and show it with your body.

When the dramatization reaches the point of conflict, call, "Stop!"

Part III:
Brainstorming of Alternatives

1. **Invite the group to suggest alternative responses to the conflict.** After you call, "Stop," lead the entire group in brainstorming ways to handle the incident differently so that the conflict is resolved in a positive way. Ask the students to think of the nine "Conflict Management Strategies" and to suggest strategies that would work in this scenario. Invite creative responses, such as combining existing strategies or offering completely new ways to approach the conflict. List responses on the board.

2. **Choose a positive alternative.** Get a consensus from the students as to which alternative ending might work best. Use this alternative as the ending for the role-play when it is reenacted.

Part IV:
Reenactment with New Ending

1. **Have the actors role-play the same scenario from the beginning up to the point of conflict.** Again call, "Stop." Then direct the actors to dramatize the positive alternative chosen by the group.

2. **Have the observers evaluate.**
While the actors are role-playing
the alternative ending, direct
the observers to evaluate its
effectiveness.

Final Discussion:

1. **Evaluate the effectiveness of
the resolution.** After the role-
play, gather the group together
and talk about whether or not the
new ending worked. If it did not
work, ask the group to select a
second alternative ending. Repeat
the role-play process, and compare
the effectiveness of the two
resolutions.

2. **Evaluate the Process.** Ask one
or more of the following questions
to stimulate thinking about the
effectiveness of the discussion and
role-play process:

   —What did you learn from this
   process?

   —What parts of the discussion
   and role-play process were the
   most valuable?

   —Why is it important to think of
   alternative endings to conflict
   situations?

   —How can practicing alternative
   resolutions to conflicts help you
   effectively handle real conflicts
   when they occur in your life?

Sharing Circle and Role-Play Topics

A Time When Someone Wouldn't Listen to Me
Sharing Circle and Role-Play Topic

Objectives:

The students will:

— acknowledge the importance of listening by describing situations in which they had to deal with the consequences of poor listening.

— focus on ways that poor listening makes conflict management more difficult.

Directions:

Begin the discussion by saying: *Today we're going to talk about the topic, "A Time When Someone Wouldn't Listen to Me."* Help the students think about the topic by saying: *Did you ever need to have someone listen to you very much, but they wouldn't do it? Tell us about the situation and how you felt at the time, without telling us who the person was.*

Repeat the topic once more before inviting the students to share their thoughts and feelings: The topic is, "A Time When Someone Wouldn't Listen to Me."

Questions for Clarification and Discussion:

1. How did you feel about the person who wouldn't listen to you?

2. When you are trying to talk and someone won't listen to you, how do you feel about yourself?

3. Why is it important to listen when you are having a conflict with someone?

4. What happens when you don't listen in a conflict situation?

At the end of the discussion, lead the class in a role-playing session, using one of the situations shared by a student during the discussion. Direct the actors to portray non-listening behavior leading to a conflict.

Something That Really Bothers Me
Sharing Circle and Role-Play Topic

Objectives:

The students will:

— express negative feelings and opinions and recognize that everyone has them.

— explain how negative feelings and thoughts can lead to conflict.

Directions:

Begin the discussion by saying: *Our topic today is, "Something That Really Bothers Me."* Help the students think about the topic by explaining: *Everyone is bothered at one time or another about something, and most of us have at least one or two pet peeves that annoy us every time they happen. I would like you to think about something that really bothers you and tell us about it. What are your emotions and how does your body feel when you have to deal with the thing that bothers you?*

Repeat the topic once more before inviting the students to share their thoughts and feelings: The topic is, "Something That Really Bothers Me."

Questions for Clarification and Discussion:

1. What similarities did you notice among the things that bother us?

2. If you could do anything you wanted about the situation you described, what would you do?

3. Do things that bother us a lot sometimes lead to conflict? How does that happen?

At the end of the discussion, lead the class in a role-playing session, using one of the situations shared by a student during the discussion. Have the actors demonstrate how the bothersome situation or pet peeve could lead to conflict.

I Observed a Conflict
Sharing Circle and Role-Play Topic

Objectives:

The students will:

— objectively discuss conflicts in which they were not involved.

— describe various ways of resolving conflict.

— compare the aftermath (feelings, consequences) of resolved vs. unresolved conflicts.

Directions:

Begin the discussion by saying: *Our topic today is, "I Observed a Conflict."* Help the students consider the topic by saying: *Think about a time when you saw two or more people in conflict. The conflict might have been verbal, where only words were used, or it might have been physical, where people hit or pushed each other. Please don't tell us the names of the people involved. Just say how the argument or fight got started and what happened.*

Repeat the topic once more before inviting the students to share their thoughts and feelings: The topic is, "I Observed a Conflict."

Questions for Clarification and Discussion:

1. How did the people involved seem to feel during the conflicts we described? How did they feel afterwards?

2. If the conflict you described was resolved, how did the people settle it?

3. How did the feelings of people who resolved their conflict compare to feelings of those who didn't?

4. How did you feel during the conflict? ...after the conflict?

At the end of the discussion, lead the class in a role-playing session, using one of the situations shared by a student during the discussion.

A Time Someone Put Me Down But I Handled It Well
Sharing Circle and Role-Play Topic

Objectives:

The students will:

— describe a criticism or rejection objectively.

— recognize their ability to maintain self-control.

— explain how put downs contribute to conflict.

Directions:

Begin the discussion by saying: *Our topic today is, "A Time Someone Put Me Down But I Handled It Well."* Help the students get into the topic by saying: *Think about a situation where you felt someone really put you down. The individual who put you down could have been an adult or a child. Perhaps the person didn't mean to do it, or maybe it was intentional. Think about what the other person said and did and describe how you felt. Then tell us what you did to handle it well. Please don't mention any names.*

Repeat the topic once more before inviting the students to share their thoughts and feelings: The topic is, "A Time Someone Put Me Down But I Handled It Well."

Questions for Clarification and Discussion:

1. How did being put down cause you to feel?

2. When you realized that you were handling the put down well, how did you feel?

3. Why do put downs so often lead to conflict?

At the end of the discussion, lead the class in a role-playing session, using one of the situations shared by a student during the discussion.

Something I Didn't Mean to Say or Do That Made Somebody Mad at Me
Sharing Circle and Role-Play Topic

Objectives:

The students will:

— describe incidents in which their behavior led to conflict.

— recognize that what they say, and how they say it, causes feelings and reactions in others.

Directions:

Begin the discussion by saying: *Our topic today is, "Something I Didn't Mean to Say or Do That Made Somebody Mad at Me."* Help the students think about the topic by saying: *We all say and do things occasionally that make other people mad at us, even though we usually don't want that to happen. Tell us about a time when you said or did something that really upset someone. The person who got angry at you could have been an adult or a child. What happened, how did you feel, and how did you react?*

Repeat the topic once more before inviting the students to share their thoughts and feelings: The topic is, "Something I Didn't Mean to Say or Do That Made Somebody Mad at Me."

Questions for Clarification and Discussion:

1. How could you tell that the other person was starting to get angry? How did the person look and behave?

2. Do you remember how you felt when you knew for sure that the person was really mad at you? What did you do?

4. Did you notice any similarities in the kinds of things that made people mad at us?

5. What are some ways that situations like these can be handled?

At the end of the discussion, lead the class in a role-playing session, using one of the situations shared by a student during the discussion.

A Time Someone Took Something Away From Me
Sharing Circle and Role-Play Topic

Objectives:
The students will:
- clarify how it feels to have something taken away.
- express negative feelings and understand that they are normal.
- describe how taking by coercion or force causes conflict.

Directions:
Begin the discussion by saying: *Our topic today is, "A Time Someone Took Something Away From Me."* Help the students think about the topic by saying: *Have you ever had something that you really liked, and an adult or a child took it away from you? The thing you liked could have been candy, gum, a special privilege or a toy, or maybe an activity, like watching a TV show or playing a game. Without mentioning names, tell us about the thing you valued and describe how it was taken away. What did you do when this was happening and how did you feel?*

Repeat the topic once more before inviting the students to share their thoughts and feelings: The topic is, "A Time Someone Took Something Away From Me."

Questions for Clarification and Discussion:
1. What did you do when something was taken away from you?
2. How did you feel when it was taken away?
3. How do you feel about the incident now?
4. Why does the act of taking away something almost always cause conflict?
5. What are some things we can do when incidents like this happen?

At the end of the discussion, lead the class in a role-playing session, using one of the situations shared by a student during the discussion.

A Time When Something I Thought Was Funny Made Someone Else Mad
Sharing Circle and Role-Play Topic

Objectives:

The students will:

— describe how positive intentions can sometimes cause negative feelings.

— explain why and how their behavior affects others.

— demonstrate how their behavior can lead directly to conflict.

Directions:

Begin the discussion by saying: *Our topic today is, "A Time When Something I Thought Was Funny Made Someone Else Mad."* Help the students think about the topic by saying: *There are many things that we think are funny. Those things make us laugh. Jokes are funny. Stories and TV shows can be funny. Sometimes we see things happen right in front of us that we think are funny. But there are some things we think are funny that make other people mad. Tell us about a time when your laughter caused someone to get angry.*

Repeat the topic once more before inviting the students to share their thoughts and feelings: The topic is, "A Time When Something I Thought Was Funny Made Someone Else Mad."

Questions for Clarification and Discussion:

1. What did the other person do or say that let you know he or she was mad?

2. After you realized the other person was mad, what did you do?

3. How did you feel when you found out the person was mad?

4. What could you have done to help the other person feel better?

At the end of the discussion, lead the class in a role-playing session, using one of the situations shared by a student during the discussion.

A Time When I Was Involved in a Misunderstanding
Sharing Circle and Role-Play Topic

Objectives:

The students will:

— explain how misunderstandings lead to conflict.

— describe how good communication can help prevent misunderstandings.

Directions:

Begin the discussion by saying: *Our topic today is, "A Time When I Was Involved in a Misunderstanding."* Help the students consider the topic by saying: *Think about a time when you had a misunderstanding with someone. The misunderstanding could have resulted from something you did or said, or it could have been due to something the other person did or said. Maybe you failed to do something that the other person expected you to do, or perhaps your perception of something was different from the other person's. Describe the misunderstanding and tell us exactly what occurred as a result.*

Repeat the topic once more before inviting the students to share their thoughts and feelings: The topic is, "A Time When I Was Involved in a Misunderstanding."

Questions for Clarification and Discussion:

1. How did the misunderstanding cause you to feel?

2. How did the misunderstanding seem to make the other person feel?

3. Why do misunderstandings so often lead to conflict?

4. If you cleared up the misunderstanding, how did you do it?

5. When you realize that you have misunderstood someone, what can you do to help clear up the problem?

6. What can you do when it appears that someone has misunderstood something you have said or done?

At the end of the discussion, lead the class in a role-playing session, using one of the situations shared by a student during the discussion.

I Was Angry at One Person, But Took It Out on Someone Else
Sharing Circle and Role-Play Topic

Objectives:

The students will:

— describe conflicts that were started by misplaced anger.

— recognize that the initial conflict may still exist even after the secondary conflict is resolved.

Directions:

Begin the discussion by saying: *Our topic today is, "I Was Angry at One Person, But Took It Out on Someone Else."* Help the students think about the topic by saying: *Our topic today is about something that happens quite a lot. Try to recall a time when you felt very angry at someone but, rather than express your anger to that person, you carried the bad feelings with you and then blew up at someone who didn't deserve it. Perhaps you were angry at a parent, a teacher, or some other adult, and were afraid to express your feelings. Or maybe you were angry at a classmate or a brother or sister. Without mentioning any names, tell us what caused you to be angry, and*

describe how the innocent person triggered your pent-up feelings.

Repeat the topic once more before inviting the students to share their thoughts and feelings: The topic is, "I Was Angry at One Person, But Took It Out on Someone Else."

Questions for Clarification and Discussion:

1. Why didn't you express your anger at the person who caused it?

2. What was the reaction of the innocent person on whom you dumped your anger?

3. When did you realize that you took out your feelings on the wrong person?

4. What are some strategies for resolving conflicts started by dumping on innocent people?

At the end of the discussion, lead the class in a role-playing session, using one of the situations shared by a student during the discussion.

A Time Someone Betrayed My Trust
Sharing Circle and Role-Play Topic

Objectives:

The students will:
— describe situations in which trust was violated.
— explain why trust is important between people.
— describe the role trust plays in conflict resolution.

Directions:

Begin the discussion by saying: *Our topic today is, "A Time Someone Betrayed My Trust."* Help the students think about the topic by saying: *Have you ever trusted a friend with something, or maybe told a person something that was a secret, and that person somehow betrayed your trust? Perhaps your secret got out, or the thing you trusted the person to take care of was damaged. Maybe the person didn't do something that you trusted would be done. Without mentioning names, tell us what happened and how you felt.*

Repeat the topic once more before inviting the students to share their thoughts and feelings: The topic is, "A Time Someone Betrayed My Trust."

Questions for Clarification and Discussion:

1. If you really want someone to trust you and you betray them just once, do you think they will ever trust you again? Why or why not?

2. Why is it important to trust a person with whom you are attempting to resolve a conflict?

3. Would you believe someone you did not trust? Would you confide in him or her? Why?

At the end of the discussion, lead the class in a role-playing session, using one of the situations shared by a student during the discussion.

I Didn't Realize That I Had Started a Fight
Sharing Circle and Role-Play Topic

Objectives:

The students will:

— recognize that conflicts are normal and can't always be avoided.

— identify behaviors that sometimes trigger conflicts.

— examine the effectiveness of different methods of responding to surprise conflicts.

Directions:

Begin the discussion by saying: *Our topic today is, "I Didn't Realize That I Had Started a Fight."* Help the students respond to the topic by saying: *Think of a time when you unintentionally said or did something that resulted in a conflict. Maybe you were one of the people involved in the conflict, or perhaps the thing you did caused other people to disagree or fight. The important thing here is that you never wanted to start a fight. Tell us what you did that started the conflict and how you reacted once it was underway.*

Repeat the topic once more before inviting the students to share their thoughts and feelings: The topic is, "I Didn't Realize That I Had Started a Fight."

Questions for Clarification and Discussion:

1. When did you first realize that something you did had started a fight?

2. What was your first reaction when the fight began?

3. If the fight started because of a mix-up or misunderstanding, how could it have been avoided?

3. What can we do to help stop or settle a conflict that we didn't mean to start?

At the end of the discussion, lead the class in a role-playing session, using one of the situations shared by a student during the discussion.

I Thought I Was Doing the Right Thing, But It Led to a Conflict

Sharing Circle and Role-Play Topic

Objectives:

The students will:

— describe situations in which ethical beliefs and actions led to conflicts.

— identify strategies to control the consequences of conflicts involving moral values/ethics.

Directions:

Begin the discussion by saying: *Our topic today is, "I Thought I Was Doing the Right Thing, But It Led to a Conflict."* Help the students think about the topic by saying: *Have you ever done something that you thought was helpful or fair or honest — something that seemed like the right thing to do — and ended up in a conflict with someone because of it? Maybe you tried to get some people to pick up their trash, or attempted to help a person who was having trouble, or told the truth in a difficult situation. Whatever the circumstances, the other person or people involved didn't like what you did and an argument or fight started. Tell us what was going on in the situation, and describe what you believed was the right thing to do and what happened when you did it.*

Repeat the topic once more before inviting the students to share their thoughts and feelings: The topic is, "I Thought I Was Doing the Right Thing, But It Led to a Conflict."

Questions for Clarification and Discussion:

1. What made you believe that what you were doing was right?

2. How did the other people involved react to what you did?

3. Do you still think your decision was right or have you changed your mind? Explain.

4. How can we control or minimize conflicts that occur when we stick to principles of right and wrong?

At the end of the discussion, lead the class in a role-playing session, using one of the situations shared by a student during the discussion.

I Got Into a Fight Because I Was Already Feeling Bad
Sharing Circle and Role-Play Topic

Objectives:

The students will:

— explain how feelings from one situation are transferred to other situations.

— identify strategies for avoiding conflicts that result from a residue of bad feelings.

Directions:

Begin the discussion by saying: *Our topic today is, "I Got Into a Fight Because I Was Already Feeling Bad."* Help the students think about the topic by saying: *This topic is about a type of experience that is very common. Have you ever been in a bad mood — feeling sad, worried, angry, or even sick — and gotten into an argument or physical fight with someone as a result? Maybe your bad feelings were because of something that happened at home or school and you lost your temper with someone who was completely uninvolved. Tell us why you were feeling bad and how the fight started.*

Repeat the topic once more before inviting the students to share their thoughts and feelings: The topic is, "I Got Into a Fight Because I Was Already Feeling Bad."

Questions for Clarification and Discussion:

1. How did you look and act when you were feeling bad? How do you think you came across to others?

2. How did the other person react when the problem started?

3. How can we avoid carrying negative feelings from one situation to other situations and people?

At the end of the discussion, lead the class in a role-playing session, using one of the situations shared by a student during the discussion.

I Got Blamed for Something I Didn't Do
Sharing Circle and Role-Play Topic

Objectives:

The students will:

— recognize that everyone is occasionally the recipient of wrongful blame.

— describe feelings and reactions that commonly result from being blamed.

— demonstrate positive methods of handling blame and resolving resulting conflicts.

Directions:

Begin the discussion by saying: *Our topic today is, "I Got Blamed for Something I Didn't Do."* Help the students respond to the topic by saying: *Most of us have had the experience of receiving blame that we didn't deserve. Think of a time this happened to you. The person who blamed you might have been a friend, parent, teacher, brother or sister. He or she thought you were responsible for something that happened — like an item getting damaged, lost, or stolen — but you were not. Tell us what you got blamed for and how you felt. Did a conflict develop? If so, briefly describe what happened.*

Repeat the topic once more before inviting the students to share their thoughts and feelings: The topic is, "I Got Blamed for Something I Didn't Do."

Questions for Clarification and Discussion:

1. What was your first reaction when you got blamed?

2. If a conflict developed, how was it finally settled?

3. How do you feel when you are blamed for something?

4. What are some things we can do to avoid getting into an argument or fight when we are blamed?

At the end of the discussion, lead the class in a role-playing session, using one of the situations shared by a student during the discussion.

I Got Involved in a Conflict Because Something Unfair Was Happening to Someone Else
Sharing Circle and Role-Play Topic

Objectives:

The students will:

— describe a conflict in which they had no initial direct interest.

— distinguish between interference and intervention.

Directions:

Begin the discussion by saying: *Our topic today is, "I Got Involved in a Conflict Because Something Unfair Was Happening to Someone Else."* Help the students consider the topic by saying: *Think of a time when you intervened in an argument or fight in order to defend someone else. You might have been trying to help a friend who was in trouble, or a younger brother who was getting beat up on, or even a person you didn't know very well. Suddenly you were right in the middle of a conflict — maybe even part of it. Without mentioning names, tell us what the conflict was about, why you got involved, and what you did.*

Repeat the topic once more before inviting the students to share their thoughts and feelings: The topic is, "I Got Involved in a Conflict Because Something Unfair Was Happening to Someone Else."

Questions for Clarification and Discussion:

1. What did you say and do when you intervened in the conflict?

2. What were the reactions of the other people involved?

3. Did the conflict get worse or better as a result of your getting involved? Explain.

4. What kinds of things can we say and do to help resolve conflicts between other people?

5. What kinds of behaviors only make matters worse?

At the end of the discussion, lead the class in a role-playing session, using one of the situations shared by a student during the discussion.

A Time When I Couldn't Understand Someone Else's Point of View
Sharing Circle and Role-Play Topic

Objectives:
The students will:

— state that every person holds unique opinions and perceptions.

— explain how opposing points of view sometimes cause conflict.

— identify strategies for avoiding or resolving conflicts caused by different perceptions.

Directions:

Begin the discussion by saying: *Our topic today is, "A Time When I Couldn't Understand Someone Else's Point of View."* Help the students ponder the topic by saying: *Think about a time when you and another person disagreed about something, and you simply could not figure out where this person was coming from. Maybe you tried hard to understand the other person's point of view, or perhaps you were so sure your own view was correct that you didn't bother to listen. Did the situation develop into a conflict? If so, how was the conflict settled.*

Repeat the topic once more before inviting the students to share their thoughts and feelings: The topic is, "A Time When I Couldn't Understand Someone Else's Point of View."

Questions for Clarification and Discussion:

1. What did you do to try to understand the other person's viewpoint? What did you do to change it?

2. What happened when you realized you were having a conflict with the other person?

3. How can people resolve conflicts caused by having different points of view?

At the end of the discussion, lead the class in a role-playing session, using one of the situations shared by a student during the discussion.

A Good Idea I Got
for Handling a Conflict
from Someone in This Group
Sharing Circle and Role-Play Topic

Objectives:

The students will:

— review specific strategies learned through discussion and role play.

— commit to using one or more new ideas or strategies when confronted with future conflicts.

Directions:

Begin the discussion by saying: *Our topic today is, "A Good Idea I Got for Handling a Conflict from Someone in This Group."* Help the students respond to the topic by saying: *In this session, I'd like you to think back over the discussions and role plays we've had, and recall one strategy or idea for handling conflict that stands out in your mind. Perhaps the strategy is one you never thought of before, or maybe you've tried it with some success and now believe you can use it much more effectively because of the experience you've gained in this group. Describe the strategy or idea, and tell us why you think it will work for you.*

Repeat the topic once more before inviting the students to share their thoughts and feelings: The topic is, "A Good Idea I Got for Handling a Conflict from Someone in This Group."

Questions for Clarification and Discussion:

1. Why did you choose this idea or strategy?

2. What similarities did you notice in the strategies we preferred for handling conflict?

3. What types of conflict does your strategy help resolve particularly well?

4. How can you remind yourself to use this strategy or idea when you are actually faced with a conflict?

At the end of the discussion, lead the class in a role-playing session, using one of the situations shared by a student during the discussion.

Training is available for...

ANGER CONTROL AND CONFLICT MANAGEMENT FOR KIDS

If your heart is in Social-Emotional
Learning, visit us online.

Come see us at
www.InnerchoicePublishing.com

Our web site gives you a look at all our other Social-Emotional
Learning-based books, free activities, articles, research, and
learning and teaching strategies. Every week you'll get a new
Sharing Circle topic and lesson.

INNERCHOICE Publishing
15079 Oak Chase Court
Wellington, FL 33414

Made in the USA
Middletown, DE
11 August 2022

71107703R00077